I0171769

IDENTIFYING THE SHIFT

DAHLIA DOYLEY

IDENTIFYING
SH**THE**IFT

ISBN: 978-1-7320944-0-6

Copyright © 2017 by Dahlia Doyley - All Rights Reserved.
IDENTIFYING THE SHIFT by Dahlia Doyley

All rights reserved under International Copyright Law. Except as
permitted under the U.S. Copyright Act of 1976, no part of this
publication may be reproduced, distributed, or transmitted in any
form or by any means, or stored in a database or retrieval system,
without the prior written permission of the publisher.

Design & Layout by Michael Matulka of Basik Studios
(www.gobasik.com) Omaha, Nebraska USA

Published by DEE - Destiny Elevate Excellence
Omaha, Nebraska USA

Printed in the United States of America

10 9 8 7 6 5 4 3 2 1

PREFACE

What type of shifts are you going through?

People with leadership qualities and bad habits have the capabilities to finish strong and win. They are truly unorganized with no direction on how to start. Although you're gifted and talented, you're the ones that I am acknowledging. The weary, but self-motivated people that endure all things that cause you pain and anger.

This is for those longing to forgive. Stop wasting precious time and energy on others with no dreams. Some of those people you're spending your time with have no desire other than destroy your destiny. The rejected ones, labeled by people, with no honor, and no respect among your peers. Your background says "no", but destiny says "yes".

Oh yes! I am calling your lazy spirit to arise. GET UP OUT OF THE STORM! It wasn't meant to kill you or cloud up your way. It was a destiny shift.

This is the book to read and store in your library. Give it to your friends. It will help them restore their dreams and visions. Identify your identity and shift!

The book of Joel Chapter: 2:25-26 states:

> [25] *I will restore to you the years that the locust hath eaten, the cankerworm, and the caterpillar, and the palmerworm, my great army which I sent among you.* [26] *And you shall eat in plenty, and be satisfied, and praise the name of LORD your GOD, and my people shall never be ashamed.*

INTRODUCTION

Hey! My name is Dahlia Doyley. I was born in Jamaica, West Indies, but spent half my life in United States. Living here has led me on a path to a better life.

At 19 years old, I found myself with child. She's my eldest, Vivianna. This was the beginning of my first shift. It's very important that you understand and identify what is taking place in your life, or for sure you'll miss it. I missed it. I can't tell you how much trouble you'll have if you're not in the place to understand when it's time to shift.

The second shift in my life (as if it weren't bad enough that I missed the first shift), happened and I missed it too. Here I am again for the second time, with child. She's my youngest daughter, Nakiya. In my mind, I wanted to the right thing; so, I got married.

Love can sometimes cloud your judgement. You have to be careful when you make decisions for your life long term. Take my word for it, it will change your whole life. And I do mean YOUR WHOLE LIFE.

After the first two shifts in my life, I came to grips with the fact that I was now the mother of two girls, two different fathers and too much on my plate. I couldn't understand why it seemed like I was the only one going through so much difficulty. I just couldn't figure it out. I decided to take another route to help myself.

You see, the trouble was that I constantly thought about what I wanted and how to get there. The only solution I had was to go to school, but with all the obstacles I was facing, school wasn't an option. I had no money, no life and little understanding as to how this country works. To make matters worse, I missed the third shift in my life, and before I knew it, the fourth shift came. It came from the left like a whirlwind picking up debris. This was the hardest time of my life.

Making decisions when children are involved can take everything out of you. I can't stress this enough. Especially when you're not sure who you are, where you're going, and what you're doing. Can you say, "identity crisis"? Been there. If any of this sounds familiar to you, you're going through identity issues.

By the time I realized I was having an identity crisis, I was in the middle of my fifth shift. I didn't see this coming. It was major movement. If I could describe it, the only word I would use is "tornado". This is the type of shift that will leave you on your face crying, snot running down your nose, broken, with only one dependent; the Lord himself.

I heard a quote from the first lady in my church while in the middle of this shift. Little did I know that those words were about to change my life and push me over the edge.

"Convenience isn't convenience if it's only for you," Lord have mercy, she did it. If you're not a believer in God, His powers, and what He's capable of, then this book probably won't help you. Then again, maybe it will, if it's true that everyone goes through at least one major shift in their life at some point.

Like I mentioned in the beginning of this book, I missed numerous shifts. It was a challenge. I was a new mother, learning how to deal with my children. I had to adjust to their mental state growing and their bodies changing. I spent time structuring their minds, teaching them how to organize, and how to handle rejection. It's important to me that I teach them to become a better woman than I was. To do this, I'm constantly checking on their future goals and accomplishments. I set an example for them by taking my generation to the next level in following my purpose. I'm setting them up on a path towards success. I'm determined to show my young ladies how to capitalize and use their gifts. They'll grow up with the power to overcome fear.

As young as my daughters were, their actions started to reveal to me that they too, were experiencing identity issues. I used simple ways to inform them about the areas of their lives so that they would understand at their age. This was my way of providing them with tools to help them to survive any identity issues they encounter as they grow. It's never too late to get the message across; no matter the age.

My purpose in writing this book was for my daughters. They're my real motivation. Recording this journal, sharing and caring for them with the opportunity to help others was my vow.

I believe that my children were given to me by God to help me fulfill my purpose on this earth, to keep me quiet and to become a better role model. It's a record of my mistakes, my turn around and re-boot. That is one of the lessons I taught my daughters.

I'm providing a book of reference, for my daughters and others, of my life journey. May this give them confidence in themselves and in God.

These are the memories of shifts that took place in my life from the age 12 through 33 recorded, signed and sealed with destiny to change lives.

CONTENTS

PREFACE i

INTRODUCTION iii

FIRST SHIFT: PERSONAL

TIME TO LEARN 1

EXPANSION 3

TIME TO LET GO 7

SECOND SHIFT: CAPABILITIES

LEARN HOW TO LOVE YOURSELF 11

MAKING MAJOR DECISIONS 15

STAND STILL 19

THIRD SHIFT: CLARITY

MOVEMENT 25

STRATEGY 29

BALANCE 33

FOURTH SHIFT: CHANGES

MINDSET 37

CAUSE AND EFFECT 41

STARTING LINE 45

FIFTH SHIFT: CHOICES

STARTING OVER 49

STUDY YOUR PATH 57

GENEROSITY AND BEING GENUINE 61

SIXTH SHIFT: COMPLETION

MAKING THE LIST... 63

PUT YOUR PLAN IN PLACE 65

LEARNING HOW TO PRAY................................67

SEVENTH SHIFT: DIRECTION

HEALTH CORPORATION................................... 73

SERVICE YOUR ENGINE..................................77

BUDGETING YOURSELF.................................. 79

EIGHTH SHIFT: FORWARD

OVERCOMING FEAR.. 83

RELENTLESS FAITH..87

RESTORATION... 93

NINTH SHIFT: DIVINE

DISCIPLINE 101

ORGANIZATION 107

THE TURNS... 113

DESTINY SHIFT: TESTING

THE SWITCH..117

THE ROUTINE BREAK.................................... 123

ADAPTATION...127

DESTINATION 131

PERSONAL
SHIFT
THE FIRST

TIME TO LEARN

As I explained in the Introduction, I missed the first shift. I was pregnant at the age of 19 with my first daughter. This was the beginning of a new chapter in my life, motherhood. Becoming a mother was the best feeling I've ever had. It was also one of the most painful experiences for me at that age. I wasn't ready for this task. This shift had me frustrated. Lord! I can't tell you how much crying I did. I had to listen as well. Here I am, observing and trying to figure out what's wrong with my newborn baby. This child was crying all the time. I didn't know what to do. I fed her, gave her baths. Nothing seemed to calm this crying child down. This was a beginning of a problem in my eyes and I didn't know how to fix it.

I didn't understand the process and that I was in a shift to begin with. This task was too much for me. I could barely care for myself and now I have a baby on my hands. I can't tell you how much I complained to my mom. I'm sure her ears bled.

I was sure this was a dream. Maybe someone could take her. I wasn't prepared for this shift, nor the learning experience. See in my mind, this was pure torture and I wanted it to stop. It had gotten so bad one night, I took the car and headed out see my mom in the middle of a snowy night. My daughter cried from Queens to Brooklyn nonstop. I needed help. I kept asking myself, "Why me?"

I couldn't do this. It took about thirty minutes to get to Brooklyn from Queens. As soon as I got there, I yelled, "MOM! COME GET DIS PICKNEY FROM ME BEFORE I LOSE MY MIND!"

For those needing translation, it meant, "Come get this child before I lose it."

As soon as I got near the door, I threw the car seat down. Before my mom could even get up the stairs, I walked away. I jumped back into my car and sped off. I drove back to my house, cursing. I told myself that I would never have another child. I was starting to feel the pressure of my decision. In retrospect, I didn't know it was a lesson. I didn't see how this would eventually help me prepare for anything in my future. All I knew, was that I was extremely tired and overwhelmed. Everything felt painful. This was the beginning of the first shift in my life and the challenges that changed me; even though I failed in preparation.

Children will bring you to realization quickly. Try to prepare yourself for the unexpected. It's not just for the preparation for children, but with other events as well. The lessons you refuse to learn, will come back. It won't go away until you master it. Before you know it, you'll be dealing with the open book test. These tests or small uncomfortable spaces will be what expands you into places of elevation. I failed and missed in this shift repeatedly. The reason was lack of preparation.

EXPANSION

Often when you hear about expansion, it's associated with money in mind. However, this is the part where it's not just about you. Preparation is a must for every step in your life. For me, it was about my immediate family and the circumstances I was about to face. I had a new venture with a new baby. It was time for me to decide. I know that I was still in the early phases of preparation, but far from prepared. Time waits on no one. Either I was going to move while I was learning or I would be waiting to exhale on a new set of challenges.

I had my new baby girl. I was renting a room from a family friend in the middle of an open book test that was meant to expand me and grow me into accepting that I was a mother with new responsibilities. Every now and then, my mom would invite me to church, but I had very little interest so I would decline. I wasn't ready for this type of expansion. This meant no sex, no parties, no drinking. In my mind, I took this as having no life. There was no way I was going to be able to do this. Surely God would be kidding if He thought I was ready. Even though I felt a strong calling of purpose on my life, I ignored it and moved on to the next problem.

Let me share a short story with you. I remember when I was 12, my mom took me to a crusade. It was an open tent, outdoor church event. I'll never forget how many people showed up to hear this one man speak. Towards the end, the speaker asked if we believe in the supernatural God. He then asked everyone that believed to raise their hands in surrender. Everyone raised their hands, so I did as well. I closed my eyes while he prayed and spoke in the name of the Jesus. All I remembered, was the sound and a different type of language coming from my mouth. I felt so powerful after the service was over that I didn't notice I was walking with my arms stiff at my side. My mom turned around and said to me, "Swing your arms," she laughed and continued, "You're going to be okay."

Little did I know, that this day would create a movement. It was the first real shift in spiritual way, because it revealed what would happen in the natural way throughout my life. I knew that there was more to me than what I was seeing in the natural sense of my life. Nine years later, at the age of 21, I was about to enter into the second shift in my life and experience God moving in a personal way for the second time since the age of 12. It was a mighty move that saved my life for sure. It expanded my view of God and showed me how real He can get, just at the mention of His name.

Truthfully, the expansion began at an early stage in my life; I just didn't understand it. I received another invitation to church and my mother delivered a message that sparked a desire to continue to go to church. In that movement, I encountered God again and felt the timing was right. This was the expansion that I needed. It was a teachable moment for me, as God was deepening my knowledge about Him; who He is, and how to connect to Him, since I missed the first opportunity.

You're never too young to learn about the existence of God. Age is nothing but a number. Put it this way, some things are bigger than your age, but you must learn it young. The Bible recorded in the Book of Samuel, how young he was when he was called by God. The fact remains that there are some things that you don't know or understand. There are also some incoming issues that can keep you from expansion. For me, it was getting to know myself. What would it be for you?

IDENTIFYING THE SHIFT

TIME TO LET GO

Finally, I thought I was going to have a life. After months of getting to know myself and seeing God expand in my life, I thought I knew enough. I'd come to a point where I thought I'd met lifetime partner. With the little knowledge I'd gained about God in that short space and time, I met a person that I liked. I had made up in my mind that we were going to have a real relationship with values, common interests, and understanding. I really thought I was ready. I was happy, smiling, putting my best foot forward. There were all these emotions with this person, but I found myself walking away from the calling on my life once again. I was pushing everyone away from my heart except this person. I was ignoring my dreams and visions. Here I was getting ready to start a new life, married. I shut out anyone and everything that I thought wasn't positive about it.

I was all about having happiness one way or another. There was no way this time wasn't a blessing. I continued with my plans, moving forward without direction, and no shame about it. But there was one problem; how could two walk together unless they agree? I can tell you for sure the answer would be NO, nope, no way.

Here I was, the day before my big office wedding, getting ready. I was overjoyed about what was happening to me. After the "I Do's" and signing of the marriage license, I stepped into the elevator to exit the building. There was a shout behind me, and before anyone could get on with me, the alarm went off. It was so loud, that I couldn't hear the people screaming on the outside giving me instructions on how to turn the alarm off. It was like a warning, but in a literal sense. I eventually got off, and didn't think much about it the rest of my day.

The following week after my wedding, I gave my heart back to the Lord. I'd made a decision to finally embrace my calling. This was only the beginning of the problem with the new purpose in my life. I wasn't sure what the call was about, how to get there, or even how long it was going to take me to understand what it was.

After my baptism a few weeks later, it felt like someone was trying to kill me. It sounded like gunshots going off in my head. It was as if there was a fully loaded M16, targeted at me, firing multiple rounds. My dreams began to reveal things. My visions became much clearer. It was like drowning in puddles of shallow water although it felt like a ocean. I felt lost. As one of the youngest (and probably the only) young lady at my church with great responsibility, I left like I didn't belong. I was met by people with perfect timing, letting me know that there is a purpose for me. It took me a while to understand what the battle in my mind was about. I had to learn how to control my thoughts and when to let go. I had to allow myself to become what I knew to be true. The battle was hard.

It meant I had to study the Word of God. To be honest, that was even harder for me to do, because I thought once I was in God, why would I need to study? I was getting the Word of God every week. Once I thought I was fine, I told myself to pay no attention to the problem. I thought it would just go away. I believed that if I just held it in, it would eventually go away at some point. The feeling to let it out had grown strong and waiting for people to accept me grew even stronger.

I spent a lot of time doing all that I thought was necessary to be "people-approved". I overlooked who they were, and undermined myself. I knew then, that it was time let it go. I was in an ongoing battle of learning how to let go. Still, I was devastated about my losses, had more responsibility on the way with my second daughter, and all I can think about was how to be accepted by people. I'd spend so much time thinking about how to make people like me for me. How do I make them understand that my outlook was coming from an experience with pain and loss? How do I explain that my body was just tired of pushing to make sure I was in attendance and supporting the cause for everyone else. All the while, I was thinking that others only saw an uneducated mother with nothing to offer.

While God was teaching me how to let go, I was busy wondering what others would, and could see. I can't help but think that maybe it was what I saw and not what others were seeing. The point when you let go is all about deciding to do it. It's not about people. It's about what you believe. It will bring you the true purpose behind it. Letting go is not just option; you do it because you must. It's the core of creating and the being of balance. Of course I missed this lesson as well, and you know I had to go through it all over again.

CAPABILITIES

THE SECOND

SHIFT

LEARNING HOW TO LOVE YOURSELF

Learning how to receive love was more challenging than I thought. Understanding what love is and recognizing it, had me confused. This lesson came with having to learn how to love me first. I had to accept me first, before I could even think about what God's love would feel like. I had to accept myself first while in transition. I had to let go of people's words and their thoughts about me.

I've found that this is a common lesson that most young ladies go through. It could simply be because we don't really understand what it is; not that we haven't seen it, we just didn't experience it ourselves. It's hard to accept real love if you've never experienced it by first loving yourself.

To understand God's love, you need to know and understand how to love yourself. How else would you believe that God's love is available to you? How does He show you who He is, until you understand loving yourself?

I was in the middle of letting go of my past, improving, and moving on with my future, when everything started to wrong. It was like I was in middle of a whirlwind. I was experiencing losses in every area of my life all over again. To me, moving forward was just a luxury word, and the word "love" (at least as I knew it), was becoming too expensive.

I faced difficulties accepting myself and loving myself enough to receive love. True love cost something, and I only knew little about it.

In the middle of learning how to receive love, I almost lost my life. Even with my visions and dreams, I still didn't trust God or understand His love. With a second child on the way, time was brewing more losses for me. I had no idea why for the second time, I was getting hit in this area. I found myself in the same place of dependency on people; not knowing if I was coming or going.

I don't know about you, but have you ever felt lost? Have you ever experienced feeling like life was playing a prank on you? Trust me when I say, it got worse. When my second baby girl decided to come a little earlier than expected because of extreme stress, this was a major problem. My body was about to give up. I'll never forget it. It was around my birthday and I was about to receive a crash course in what love was all about.

I woke up on the morning of my birthday, entering my third trimester. I wasn't feeling very well. My feet were swollen and I felt very sick. I started to see spots before my eyes. "This must be a vision," I told myself, but spots? My feet looked like oranges were growing on the sides of them. I figured out quickly that this wasn't a vision and I needed attention, fast.

I got to the emergency room quickly. My doctor, who was supposed to be off that day decided to work a double shift. She spotted me in the corner of the waiting room. She called out to me and asked, "Why are you here? I just saw you at the health center." Before I could answer, my tongue got heavy and I could barely speak. I was in middle of a mild stroke. "How long have you been here?" she asked. I responded with, "Around 20 minutes." She took my vital signs and I remember seeing her flash her hands across my face. "What's wrong?" I heard her ask. "I'm seeing spots," I reply to her slowly. Shortly after I was rushed off to surgery.

I woke up in the ICU with no baby in my stomach, my arms slightly deformed, and in a battle for my life. I knew that day, that God was on my side. I received His gift of love that day. He was with me and I felt it. Some things are not coincidence. The doctor decided to stay after doing a double shift. She took a glance at me at the right moment. I know you're thinking that maybe it was just my lucky day.

You see, I don't believe in luck. I believe in moments such as this one, being divinely orchestrated by God. After I put myself through hell trying to find love, I finally understood love. On this day, I understood love. Does luck work like this? It was just my luck that day to be feeling ill? Just my luck to have my doctor (who was supposed to be off) taking care of me? Just my luck that she glanced in my direction in the waiting room to see me in the corner after being ignored by other doctors? That day, I accepted myself and loved myself enough to live. God's love was much more present.

Bad judgment can cause you pain in your life or to lose your life completely. Protect yourself always, especially the matters of your heart. Those are major decisions that change lives. Think carefully about some of the things that happened in your life that caused you great pain. How did your decisions contribute to that and how did it make you feel afterwards?

Now that you understand the importance of decision-making and the way it can change your life, use that to help you create a space for the next great decision or adventure. Use it as a positive tool, even if the situation feels horrible. Facing it will help you overcome the fear of it. Yes, it can be hard and bring back some painful memories, but the sooner you do, the better your future decisions will be.

MAKING MAJOR DECISIONS

There comes a time in your life where you'll have to make major decisions. Boy, was I in the wrong neck of the woods. This was the time I needed every word coming from God. I didn't care who He used to share it. After overcoming and regaining full function of my body after suffering a mild stroke, I needed to be fed with positive words. I was hoping to find it in church on Sunday after praise and worship, tithes and offerings. Surely, I did.

My pastor spoke two words while speaking from the book of Ruth, "Stand still." The pastor shared with us the love of two ladies Ruth and Naomi. The love and loyalty between these ladies compelled Ruth to make a decision toward her mother in-law that would change both of their lives. This decision brought both ladies back to Naomi's hometown after both women suffer great losses. Naomi was somewhat bitter and confused after her losses. While Naomi was well known among the people, Ruth was heard of in the nearby areas. Ruth's decision to be faithful to Naomi, led her to discovering a blessing. It wasn't just any blessing, but a threefold blessing. Arriving just in time for harvest. Naomi had an influence on Ruth's decision.

Sometimes, when it comes to a major decision you need to find someone with great influence. Someone who has your best interest at heart to help you, someone with a strong relationship with you and God. Loyalty has its rewards. Consider Ruth, who was blessed because of her loyalty.

When I heard that message I had a couple of major decisions to make. To stay where I was, or go back to my home country outside of the United States. I was tired and missed my family. Besides, it was so cold in the United States and Jamaica is so warm. My thoughts went up and down between staying or going. I was in turmoil. I was too determined to walk in my purpose and was looking for reasons to rationalize why it was okay for me to walk into failure. Destiny has ways of teaching you who the real boss is. It was funny, but every time this specific decision came about, a family member would invite me to come over to fellowship.

There are sometimes in decision-making that you'll need to stand still and wait for the right time to move, especially when you're not sure. The Book of Ruth became a foundation for answers to my questions whenever I needed clarity on dealing with something personal. It was my reference alongside the Book of Esther. I realized loyalty comes with a price and you can be hurt if you're loyal to the wrong people.

God showed me how loyal He is to His people. That message brought me favor and blessings because I decided to stay where I was. A few years later, I was in a place to receive all that God had promised me, including a threefold blessing for standing on His loyal words.

It took me years to understand why I should wait and the reason why it was important. It's never easy to wait on anything when you got options. Typically when you're making decisions, it's always about you. Be careful of the path you take. Use principles that are true and will guarantee you full results. As you live, you'll make some brave moves in the name of loyalty, but be careful of people that you show your loyalty to. Not everyone understands the value of this word. You'll be broken and upset if your naive about it. Practice loyalty to yourself first and if you can treat yourself right, then dealing with others and knowing where you stand won't be a problem.

IDENTIFYING THE SHIFT

STAND STILL

Staying focused is easier said than done. When you focus on people, the enemy can keep you in an obsessive-repetitiveness to string you along. It can keep you from having joy, and you'll find yourself going downhill faster than you know.

I practiced loyalty with the people I knew, but just when I thought I was getting better in my decision-making, I found myself in need of rescuing. To my surprise, there wasn't a loyal person to be found. Even though I had just learned about loyalty, I was still getting it wrong. I had crossed the line of loyalty into obsession. When you become obsessed with the people you know, you'll follow them everywhere blindly over a cliff.

I couldn't figure out. It was a love/hate relationship that I didn't understand and processing the information on my heart was too much. The problem was that I had become so obsessed in pleasing people. I wasn't reading enough to grasp a full understanding of what in the heaven was happening to me. I felt hollow inside, like my heart was barely beating. I lost my focus and my heart shifted to the bottom of my feet. I was a shell; a walking dead person, even though I was in church.

Staying focused was a challenge for me. My head felt like a brick, and I was trying to balance the brick to keep it from tipping over. My heart was in a state of desperation and my brain felt like gelatin. It took me awhile to understand that learning was not the issue I faced, but rather retaining the knowledge I received. It wasn't the people. It was me forgetting what I'd learned and how to stand still and know

God. That meant stop trying to do things by myself, but to also stop seeing people as a rescue squad.

God was once again, on time, sending me another word to help revive my heart. The message was "Take off the D.N.R (Do not resuscitate)." It came from my Senior Pastor, Pastor Yvonne Shaw. This message impacted me with such force and gave me the strength to return to my position of standing still and focusing. This was like surgery for me. It was major. What this message said to me, was to do whatever it takes to keep my heart beating, please resuscitate.

The struggles in my life were real and the shame I faced, a young mother with two children, two separate fathers, and a failed marriage left my heart in deep pain. The disappointment had it barely beating. I was in bad shape internally. I was constantly depressed and worried about my future. What was the point of all of this? I asked myself this question repeatedly. I was so grateful for that message especially when I wasn't reading my Word enough, those words helped me to maintain my stand.

Maintaining your stance in the time when you feel disoriented isn't easy, but if you can survive the initial trauma it will become a lesson applicable for future situations. Oftentimes you have to face the effect of the actions made by you. Don't forget that the enemy's plan is to distract you and keep your mind in a useless state of obsession and depression. All of his devices are there to interrupt any progress you make, detouring you into the wrong direction, suppressing and oppressing you. Understand that over time, you can recover with the hope that your wrong turn would be just what you need to land you on the correct path.

What does "stand still" mean to you, fear or favor? It really depends on how you look at it. If you allow God to be present in your decision-making you'll find favor in every area of your life. Without His input, fear will keep you in failure.

The Bible talks about favor in standing still. In the Book of Joshua, he spoke to the sun commanding it to stand still in the middle of a battle (Joshua 10:12-13).

> *12 Then spake Joshua to the Lord, in the day the Amorite, before the children of Israel, sun, stand still upon Gibeon and, thou moon in the valley of Aj-aron.*
>
> *13 and the sun stood still, and the moon stayed, until the people had avenged themselves upon their enemies, is not this written in the book of Ja-sper? So, the sun stood still in the midst of heaven, and hasted not to go down about a whole day.*

Joshua acknowledged God and spoke a word. God was present in this act. Joshua had a relationship with the Father and gained access into His presence. The sun and the moon obeyed his words.

There may be times in the middle of a battle that you'll just need to stand still. Believe it or not, standing still is also an action.

The point is, there are moments in your life where you'll have to wait and see what God is trying to show you. Wait on His presence to guide you. Don't fall into people-pleasing. Fall into God's Word. Get direction from Him and

He will teach you when to stand still, and when to speak.
He will deliver you out of any circumstance. You just must
learn how to stand still.

**STAND STILL IN THE MOMENTS
WHEN NO ONE ACCEPTS YOU.**

**STAND STILL WHEN YOUR DREAMS
AND VISIONS DON'T MAKE SENSE.**

**STAND STILL WHEN YOUR WORLD
CRUMBLES BENEATH YOU.**

**STAND STILL WHEN YOU CAN'T SEE
YOUR WAY OUT OF THE DARK.**

**STAND STILL WHEN YOUR FRIENDS
BECOME YOUR ENEMIES.**

**STAND STILL WHEN YOU FEEL LIKE
YOU HAVE LOST YOUR SANITY.**

**STAND STILL ON GOD'S WORD OF
TRUTH AND LIGHT.**

CLARITY
SHIFT
THE THIRD

MOVEMENT

This shift was a combination of three lessons. Movement, strategy, and balance. At this point, learning to love myself , maintaining my stand, and prioritizing my decision-making became a picnic basket in comparison to the lessons I missed too many times. It took me awhile to understand the reason why I needed to be in movement and what it meant. There are some things that require you to stand still in movement; work while you wait. Other things require you to rely on God. This lesson was different, and my outlook on what movement was, was a total disaster. I thought that if I was in movement, then people would see me changing the way I dressed and how adoring my children was top priority. I was in movement with my outside appearance.

While taking care of my children and myself were good for my image, I was still missing the value of the lesson. What did movement mean to me? What part of my life needed the most attention internally? What would take me into a stable and consistent outside? I was finally comfortable in my own skin and taking a leadership role in my own life. I found myself in a place where nothing bothered me, on the outside at least. I had a strategy for the outside, but still needed help on the inside with balance.

I was tone deaf when it came to fixing the one thing that would bring me fulfillment in my life. I was suppressing things inside, but building on the outside. I didn't understand that I was covering up my feelings. Soon after, I realized that I was missing the vertical and horizontal structure to keep my foundation on the inside successful enough to, let that illuminate success on the outside. This was when I saw movement in a new light. The problem was that I was in movement, just on the wrong area of my life. What does movement mean you? Movement can be an open door, healing, a blessing, or something you need to fix. Movement can shift you into a different place right in that moment. Now let me share my experience of healing. This was a pivotal moment that changed my life for the better.

I received a healing in this lesson and I thank God for it. I was about to turn 28 and God delivered me through His Word, from a deep depression. I don't know if you believe in dreams, but usually when I receive a dream, it takes some time for it to happen. This time, it took just a few days. The dream gave me four numbers, 2028. I went back and forth with myself on what these numbers meant. I prayed about it with concern.

Later, I was watching a television program on the Word Network and the gentleman repeated the number 28. He spoke about the number 28 and what it meant about future things. After listening carefully, I didn't know how to process it. I didn't fully understand what I'd just heard. I felt discouraged and worried because it sounded like he was speaking concern for the year 2028. The next morning, I got up and started getting myself ready for church. I heard, "2028 is here."

It sounded like I was talking to myself for a split second, but I felt a movement in my mind, a shift, like water covering my head.

That Sunday was my birthday. I turned 28 on that day, so this part made sense to me. The true meaning of the numbers 2028 revealed to me. The calendar year was 2011. The dream revealed that this number 2028, meant that we're now in the 20th century, in the year 2011, on my 28th birthday, after I had received healing from the spirit of depression. It turns out that 2028 was about my 28th birthday, and a deliverance took place in my life that day. It was right on time and just what I needed.

The following week, I recall reading about an experience in the book of Matthew where a woman received a healing for an issue of blood. She'd heard word that Jesus Christ was in her neighborhood. As He was passing down the street, she went after him, touched His garment, and immediately received her healing. She was in movement when she received her deliverance.

The point I'm trying to get across is that nothing just happens. Don't be afraid to move. Movement can bring spiritual manifestations in your life. Be ready for these things to happen, as well as the movement you make in the natural. It can all be for your benefit. This the area of your life that can cause fear. Why? Because it has to move when you move.

IDENTIFYING THE SHIFT

STRATEGY

To have a good strategy is important wouldn't you say? Prioritizing your moves can bring you great results. In this lesson, I decided to try and start my own business. I just knew I was ready. With a little marketing and very few relationships with people, I started out on a new adventure. I was hoping that everyone would see the change and take some interest in me. I started a business selling makeup to people in my age bracket. The only problem was that a majority of people I knew, knew very little of me. I only received a handful of customers who saw my ambition and showed me pity. At this point, I needed someone to help me pull this business together.

My daughters were still extremely young, and the country was going through a recession. I struggled with finding a job to supplement my business. I was motivated, so I thought I'd bring my business to the internet to see how much I could communicate with and build more relationships outside of the few people I knew. I found it to be much harder than I thought. I had to accept that my makeup venture wasn't working out. Although this was my first business attempt and I was very enthusiastic about it, I was also disappointed about it not going as well as I had planned. I knew I needed a lot more help from people with knowledge in business and strategy.

After around a year more of trying it my way, nothing was positive was happening, so I gave up. Later that summer, I decided to give a new business in the travel industry, a try. I named the business Victorious Travels Agency. With no hesitation I started it up, and within the first few months,

I got a few people on as clients. It seemed like it was going to work out long term.

Sure enough, it was short lived. My clients would go on their vacation, but they were making a lot of complaints. I didn't know how to handle these situations. It was harder than selling makeup, but I wanted to be better. I started taking some classes online to learn about the different airlines, cruise ships and destinations. It was well worth it, but I came out of it telling myself that it was going to take extreme marketing, business etiquette, relationship-building, research, information downloading and connections.

After the classes I started to understand why my makeup business was an epic failure. I took a great loss in this adventure but learned a lot about strategies for my next business. These are some of the major strategies I learned:

MARKETING [Noun]
The action or business of promoting and selling products or services, including market research and advertising.

ETIQUETTE [Noun]
The customary code of polite behavior in society or among members of a profession or group.

RELATIONSHIP [Noun]
The way in which two or more concepts, objects, or people are connected, or the state of being connected.

RESEARCH [Noun]
The systematic investigation into and study of materials and sources to establish facts and reach new conclusions.

INFORMATION [Noun]
Facts provided or learned about something or someone.

People, places, and things are used to create shifts in your life. People are very important for a business relationship. Proper etiquette is a major communication tool, which helps you to receive proper information, and research will launch you into a successful business. This is what I've learned in the attempts of starting my own business and failing. I think in business, a paradigm shift is needed to change your mindset with people you meet. The shift helps you recognize the places you need to go and the things you need to get there.

IDENTIFYING THE SHIFT

BALANCE

After many months of continuing to work on my business, doing all the things I mentioned above, I started to feel another side of entrepreneurship...the stress! I was constantly tired, missing my online classes, and still trying to work with my daughters. It was a lot! I compared it to working five jobs.

I was putting a lot of work in, but was still struggling. My dreams of becoming a business owner were a nightmare. Loss of vision, blockage, losing focus. I felt like a failure. I complained every day. I was becoming impatient and was soon ready to quit. I was in a familiar place of needing balance in my life.

It's important for any person that has a dream or vision to have balance. It's also very important to use your time wisely. I got a calendar to help me balance and keep myself on tasks. I created a routine that worked well with my time. Let me give you an example of what I mean about creating a routine calendar.

My day begins with praying, between five or six a.m. I set the atmosphere before I go to work. After prayer, I head out to get into the other parts of my day. I work for about twelve hours for maybe three or four days straight. This is why it's so very important to balance. Now that I have a family to take care of, after I get home from work (a little after 7pm), I finish up dinner for everyone. I spend about an hour enjoying their company before settling down. I read a bit before falling asleep.

On my days off, I would schedule going to the gym and other activities that I'm not able to do during my long work days. I was stabilizing myself to accomplish a specific goal and desires that I designed for my life. There is no greater feeling than reaching the purpose of your day. Balancing your work and business to get you to your destination, organizing all area of your life would be a major plus to your daily life. This also includes balancing your health, diet, and the children. Your body is your temple so keep yourself in shape with plenty exercise and rest. Make sure you get the full amount of sleep that your body needs to function. Organization is not just about your body and business, it's also about your finances.

This is a journey that most of us give up on because we don't have the tools we need. Some of us just continue with what we've learned. Having healthy credit and money to invest is a must. I learned how to do both things after watching an online program called "The Budgetnista". It led me to finding more information on IRAs, investing, building good credit, and how to teach your children to save. It had to slap me in my face for me to get it. Honestly, I would've faced it later if I didn't get started. I was at least $300,000 behind in retirement. I was the only breadwinner for my household, so it was time for me to get busy. What better way to start than by balancing my checkbook, watching my spending, paying down debt and putting away a little more.

Whether you're an entrepreneur or not, balancing your life can bring you great results and success. It helps to keep you focused on time lost and gained. Staying aligned with your calendar is crucial to your balance, if you act on it and stick to it. It won't be easy. Having extra support and sorting out your time throughout the day is very beneficial.

Remember, it's all about fixing your lifestyle to your comfort and surroundings.

Applying daily balance is extremely necessary. Movement, strategy and balance are all connected. Trust me, the struggles and discomfort in achieving balance is worth it. Some of the most well-known feelings in this shift will determine whether you're going to experience a detour. You'll have to recognize these detours and take the avenues that encourage you to make great changes, if you want to have success.

The detour is a personal "work-on-me" area. It can sometimes be a personality defect in your attitude or behavior toward balance your life. This the part where we mostly complain. It can get a little hard because it's something new. Watch over your own personality traits. Pay attention to who you are and this will launch you forward without experiencing a longer period in a detour. Practice awareness with your immediate family to adjust. They'll help you notice any personality differences. The bottom line to this shift is for you to understand who you are. Make an intentional effort to interrupt any identity issues that may be masking with your personality to balance yourself.

CHANGES

SHIFT THE FOURTH

MINDSET

What words will change your mind?

As an entrepreneur in the making, words mean a lot to me. I'm always listening to hear positive and influencing words or phrases to speak to my clients. By now you can tell that I go to church often. I find that a positive word can change my outlook on life. It can change how I deal with people, complex business decisions, and personal issues.

One Sunday, I received another life-changing quote. When you receive something that will change your life, your feelings will change. It's so funny that earlier that morning, I didn't even want to go, but I pushed through and went to church that Sunday.

I'll never forget these words because of the week I'd had. The words made me think about my character and what I needed to change. They came from my First Lady and Senior Pastor Yvonne McDonald, "Convenience isn't convenience if it's only for you."

Although the words were requoted, it changed my life coming from her lips after one of the most difficult weeks I'd had. I was trying to work a business and babysitting to make extra money on the side to help support my family.

I know that everyone may interpret these words in their own way depending on what is happening in their lives. The word "patience" found me in this quote. It consumed me with tears and compassion. Even though I was a sitter for other people's children, it wasn't just about the money, but about the trust that I developed with their children that taught me patience in being inconvenienced.

I wasn't making enough to help my family, but I was giving myself to others and learning at the same time a valuable lesson that would lead me into my identity. It was desperately needed for the journey ahead.

The definition of patience took me by surprise in this quote. It wasn't because I hadn't heard the word before, but it was nowhere to be found in my life.

PATIENCE: implies, enduring, waiting, as a determination of the will and not simply under necessity. As such it is an essential Christian virtue to the exercise which there are many exhortation, we need to wait patiently for God, to endure uncomplainingly the various forms of suffering, wrong and evil that we meet with, bearing patiently injustices which we cannot remedy and provocations we cannot remove.

Learning patience can be difficult, but necessary. I was learning patience and inconvenience, and seeing how they walk hand in hand. They were applied very similarly in both lessons that I learned, and at the same time, I could see God's patience for people in His character traits. If you're a believer like I am, then this should make sense to you.

Romans 15:5 spoke of the God of patience:

> [5] *Now the God of patience and consolation grant you to be likeminded one toward another according to Christ Jesus.*

This lesson was big. It impacted my character and taught me true patience. It showed me how being inconvenienced can build you in many ways.

I have a small exercise I'd like you to try. These are just a few questions that I ask myself to keep me accountable for my daily growth and the things I can change to walk into my identity as an individual.

HAVE YOU BEEN IN PATIENT WITH YOUR LOVED ONES?

YES / NO

HAVE YOU EVER RECEIVED PATIENCE FROM ANYONE?

YES / NO

DO YOU THINK PEOPLE IN YOUR LIFE DESERVE YOUR PATIENCE?

YES / NO

DO YOU EXERCISE PATIENCE?

YES / NO

HOW PATIENT DO YOU WANT GOD TO BE WITH YOU?

YES / NO

Patience is an eight-letter word with great impact in your life. It is a processing word, bringing you to a complete pause in your personal walk. If you're not careful, you can ruin your chances at anything you set out to do in your life without applying some level of patience. You must practice patience to be able to minister to your family, friends, and enemies. Without patience, you will experience side effects in your life and health. Tiredness, fatigue, high blood pressure, and other health issues can enter your life because you have no patience. Have you ever heard the phrase, "Patience is a virtue?" It takes practice for you to get there. Fully engage yourself with patience; encourage and identify with it.

CAUSE AND EFFECT

How would it affect you in your life?

The key ingredient to the, "Convenience isn't convenience," quote, is patience. I'll admit that patience affected me in ways that irritated me during this shift change. Now that I understood why being inconvenienced was a great lesson to learn and seeing that it's not only for me, I should've known that I was about to go through a practice test with my family. I had to exercise what I was learning with my own family.

It's so funny that you have more patience with people outside of your family, but not enough for yourself or your family. This was going to be a test to see if I really understood the true meaning of that quote. I was starting to think trouble had taken a vacation from my life and yet, there it was. A sudden sickness on an old injury that took down one of my family members. It was about to take my whole family to a different level and bring a whole new meaning to side effects.

It was around my eighth year living with my parents supporting me and my two daughters. The storm hit us head on with the loss of half our income and relying on each other back and front. After a couple of weeks, patience went through the door and inconvenience was too much for all of us.

My mom's back injury was relentless. As the week went by, this was a true test that awakened us to the reality of who our true friends were. Although income wasn't the only loss, we soon discovered that all the work we had put into our friendships meant nothing. It was challenging to watch my mom cry daily. She described the back pain, like a worm eating out her back. My eyes swelled with tears as I called on Jesus to help.

This was a challenge that we couldn't afford. It was time to gird up my loins and I wasn't prepared. We had bills to pay and only one income. Then, this storm started to rock the boat. We owed piles of money. When my patience became impatience, it showed us who the real boss was in every area of our life. I started to see the God we serve in very different light.

Impatience has no limits and doesn't care if you're sick or inconvenienced. I became a chef in food preparation for the sick, making sure that my mom would eat healthy. I also had to see to it that she was ok while my dad worked to keep us above the high stormy water of bill collectors. We started to eat small portions of food. Surprisingly, we were full every day and even more content even though we were going through serious financial issues. The lesson had a greater impact than I ever knew.

Whenever you're going through a family matter, illness or any other problem, treat it as if you're in the position of the person depending on you. There comes at least once in life, when you're going to need patience and will inconvenience someone. Just know that every lesson or situation you learn it, is worth it.

Having some tolerance in your life will bring you good opportunities to learn more about yourself. It'll better you when it comes to dealing with loved ones, friends and especially your adversary. The effects can be great or small when the boat that you're rowing loses an engine and you lose momentum. Being inconvenienced for a little while can build your character and teach you real patience. Your real potential is brought to life in these temporary situations.

Going through this difficult time with my family brought me to a point of gratitude. The situations we encountered made us so strong and challenged me to make changes. You'll never know when the experience you have will come into play again. Each time it does, you'll learn something new about yourself. Experiences can sometimes feel like an ocean, but understand that this is just shallow water teaching you how to stand. If only we could understand the significance of changes and how real they are for your life, whether you're prepared or not, you'll be affected. It's how you learn that will cause a greater effect on you and your identity.

IDENTIFYING THE SHIFT

STARTING LINE

Where do you start?

I had to ask myself where did I want to start making the changes that affected me, and what could I do better the next time unexpected trouble arrive? What if I was the only breadwinner? How could I prepare myself for the next test? What if the shoe was on the other foot and I was ill? Who could I rely on? What measures could I take to prepare my finances to cover these gray areas where money is one of the most important functions for my family?

After my mom felt better and was taking baby steps to walk after almost three months of bed rest with her back injury, I had to make some decisions. Patience and convenience was lost and it was a bigger issue that I thought. Starting over was the best thing for me to do in this situation. I started a new partnership with myself, and I was excited about it. Life was looking good again. I had new info and identity issues that were within in my reach to fix and work on.

One of things you must be able to do when trying to figure where to start is to identify where you are, and how it affects you in every way. Even though I knew and understood the importance of why I should try to fix these areas, I was prone to make mistakes because I had no support system.

Things were about to turn from bad to worse. I went crazy. I ended up running the streets with an, "I don't care," attitude. I was out of control, going to every party and drinking every liquor I knew. I literally dropped off. I didn't know what do. It took me about a year to figure out what was happening to me. I was about to leap into my 30th birthday and I had nothing, nothing, nothing. I was discouraged about all the damages that happened. I wondered how different the outcome would have been if it had been me. The recession came and left and I wasn't affected by it because I had nothing.

This was a reality I didn't want to face. After I calculated where I was in my life, and the number of things I had to do and learn, I realized how much I had inconvenienced my parents.

I remember the day I turned thirty. There was a convention going on at church that night. I was at my lowest point. I left church before it was over even though this was the place I got the last encouraging words from. I was hurt, disappointed, and discouraged.

Figuring out where to pick up and start again can be overwhelming for many reasons. Whether you understand what you're going through not, starting over won't work when you're only relying on yourself. Failure to ask for help can lead you on an up and downhill path, distracting you from your purpose.

Discouragement and disappointment are some of the feelings you can have while changing and building on what you need to learn about yourself. Think about what you want to accomplish. Understand that these feeling happen because it's personal to you and your growth. Be on the lookout when you shift in personality, the people you hang with, and places you go. It's ok to be patient with yourself in these times. Ask someone you trust for prayer and guidance because it will be hard to trust your own decision with these emotions.

CHOICES

SH/IFT

THE FIFTH

STARTING OVER

Giving yourself a fresh start can be rewarding if your decision-making and choices become better. How would you know it's time for a fresh start and when to cut all the strings attached to circumstances beyond your control? What past choices can you use as a reference point? You need to determine that. You'll have to think through what, who, and where, you're going to be. Use facts about your life that will help you make those choices easier. Listing the pro and cons can help you get clarity and results. These are some of the questions I asked myself when I decided it was time for a fresh start. It's vitally important that you know where you're going, and to question yourself about the path you're going to take; especially if children are involved.

WHAT ARE YOU GOING TO DO
TO MAKE YOURSELF BETTER?

WHO CAN YOU TRUST
ON THIS NEW PATH?

WHERE DO YOU START
ON THIS JOURNEY?

Often, these questions may bring you to feelings because of losses. You can lose people and move to a new place at any given time. Give yourself space and time to answer the questions and plan. The purpose and real reason for you to do this is to fulfill your dreams and visions. It's time to embrace what you failed at and misunderstood, to put it to practice for a better life.

After many losses, including your identity and dignity, you have nothing left to lose. Give it all you've got. Take on the clear blue sky and make your eagle wings fly both spiritually and naturally.

It's critical that you listen to a professional in your field of business. Trust me when I say that the right people are before your face if you pay attention. Be sure to listen and keep notes in this new beginning. Read over your notes with understanding and ask questions when you don't. Before you make a move, utilize all the spare time you have and dedicate yourself to your success.

This is where people become an asset. It doesn't matter if they like you or not. Keeping relationships will help to benefit any opportunity coming your way. Let you character show. Familiarize yourself with people that understand and have experience in the areas you've struggled with. Use their wisdom as references and guidelines to became teachable.

Now that we know that starting over is what to do, let's talk about the road to success and the addition to a new lesson you'll need to learn. Imagine you're driving a car, bike, or you're on foot. The point is to use your imagination.

Say you're making a right turn at the end of a road ahead. The arrow instructs you to keep right. This is the first sign of the shift in driving after all the information you gathered.

Up ahead at the second turn, the arrow changes its shape. Go straight ahead and keep your eyes on the speed limit. Stay on the path, the arrows are making sense. All you need to do is follow the signs and make the right turn.

The next turn alerts you slow down a little because it's a winding road. It brings you into a different feeling on your journey. You stay cautious and watch your speed limits. Speak less and keep limited number of people around you to avoid any type of manipulation or deception on this road.

This next turn, will be based on your ability to watch out for manipulation and deception. It can become a mess, and you could be thrown off the road eventually ending up at a dead end, because you can't really predict the signs that are around the corner. The problem with these types of signs, is that they take more time to regroup when you miss your turn and get ready for the turnaround. Before we continue, let's talk about the elephant that got you here.

MANIPULATION: Being under this influence can feel like a deadly hold on your throat. You can't breathe. It's contagious and addictive, driving you to keep wanting more. You find yourself driven by other people's motives, concepts, and fears. Manipulation can, and will make you feel unwanted. You'll look for ways to be wanted by your manipulators. This is how you arrive at a dead end on the road to success. It gets curvy and you could miss your turn being under this influence.

Manipulation has feelings attached to it. The cutting feelings of pain, anger, feeling trapped and wrapped up in making decisions. They become more difficult and complex. Manipulation feels a lot like an invasion in your mind. Your thoughts are not clear without opinions of your manipulators. You're too dependable on wanting to be perfect for their approval. These are some of the signs you need to look out for when you're starting over on your journey or rebuilding.

One of the most dangerous things about manipulation is how you deal with it. The confusion in your mind that comes from being manipulated can cause you to lose hope and confidence in yourself.   You could lose years from your journey toward your purpose and destiny. You have to look out for the warning signs. There are usually red flags that tell you there's a problem, raising concern about the people you're around.

Manipulative people are usually very jealous. They 'll lead you away from the people you should trust. They'll fill your head with their opinions, damaging your relationships with others to make you confused. Isolate yourself, your decisions concern others. They also have a bully mentality. They're very sly about their responses to you and will use reverse psychology. Betrayal from them comes easily, and they're quick to call you names with the intent to damage your character with mutual acquaintances. Their identity is masked to cover up by their manipulative personality traits, showing care toward you to gain your trust.

 There's a story from the Bible almost everyone knows, regarding how Judas betrayed Jesus for money. Judas was manipulated, and his decision sent Christ to the cross. Sometimes we're easily manipulated to the point that we betray the people that love us. Could this be coming from an identity issue that you're facing?

Judas lost his life in a middle of a battle he took upon himself. He refused to be transformed and separated from the thing that as keep him hostage; allowing himself to be manipulated by his past failures and theft.

Judas was a follower of Christ. Notice, that the purpose of Christ didn't change. When you understand the manipulation and people who use it, it will be easier to continue your path toward fulfilling your purpose and destiny.

DECEPTION: Deception is different from manipulation in some ways. You may hear people define deception as a snake or as sneaky behavior. I agree.

A snake is very sly and dangerous. To be sly, is to have or show a cunning and deceitful nature; very dishonest and underhanded; sneaky. The difference with deception is that it cannot be hidden for long. It will find a way to show up.

Deception can look like an unnaturally shaped snake. You'll have trouble if you can't recognize it in the spiritual. It's too hard to see it in the natural form from a person. Deception can be dispelled if you treat it with calmness and willpower. If you can understand the nature of what deception brings, you can deal with it when it comes your way. Deception can be a small thing with the potential to becoming a larger problem depending on the history of the person. It cannot be hidden for long before you notice it. Noticing it is one of the first ways to start untangling yourself from deceptive people. You must understand that keeping focus while on this road to purpose and destiny is of gigantic importance. Those arrows are there for your future.

Let me give you a small example of how I learned about the mind of deceptive people. Deceptive people are usually the first ones to about other people. Drilling information from you and wanting you to pick a side. They'll test you to see where your mindset is. They'll ask you questions, keep their business a secret, but call you to find out yours. Now if you're an open person like I am, deceptive people see you as an easy target. They'll play with you for a long time and at this point, you need to decide what you'll do. You can learn how to deal with deceit or stay completely away if you're not sure what it is or how to identify it. Like I said earlier, on this road you'll have to be careful. Purpose and destiny have two different meanings that can have a great impact on your life and others.

Here's an exercise that helped me to walk out of manipulation and deception.

Write down any time you can remember being manipulated or deception happened to you. I want you to read it over once, then discard of it in your own way. I burned mine. I understand that it's easier said than done. This will help you to get to the next arrow, turn around, reverse from the dead end, and move forward.

As you head back on the winding road, the feeling of unstableness will occur. Look through the rearview mirror and say goodbye to the past pain and hurt. Use your windshield wiper to remove the rain (translation: wipe the tears from your eyes). Turning around can make you feel lost, but you're still the driver of the vehicle. The road has curves that aren't visible, but you survived the dead end that was designed for manipulation and deception. The setback meant to kill your purpose, but God! He's always looking out for you and making you stronger. You'll be more alert to false information.

One of the most daring deceptions I read in the Bible was in the book of Esther 1:10-22. The king was deceived and lost his wife and then proceeded to put the kingdom's business out in the streets. To make matter worse, he sent out a decree that all the wives must take care of their husband, even if it meant the women would be humiliated like he did to his wife Vash-ti. Most people who argue that Vash-ti disobeyed her husband and deserved the punishment of being banished from the place she called home. She lived for years serving her king and husband, but tell me what decent woman would want to be paraded around in front of drunken men? When I read the full text, I saw how the king was deceived and dismissed his wife from the palace she called home.

WRITE YOUR EXPERIENCES OF BEING MANIPULATED.

SHARE YOUR EXPERIENCES WITH BEING DECEIVED.

IDENTIFYING THE SHIFT

STUDY YOUR PATH

This lesson will help throughout the rest of your life, business, and friendships with people that cross your path. Studying your path can have you change locations. You may have to rely on others to make it happen. Getting plenty of information and doing your research is a big necessity to have before success in this move.

Most of what you take on this move is not a necessity for you to survive. You can't bring all your belongings, or your family and personal issues with you. This part of the process will break down and rebuild where you're going. Remember, you've done your research and know the signs. You'll be well on your way to being fully restored. Studying will teach you about generosity and genuineness with those who cross your path. The definition of generosity from Webster's dictionary puts it this way.

GENEROSITY: The quality of being kind, understanding, and not selfish; the quality of being generous especially, willingness to give money and other valuable things to others.

In this definition, quality make sense because what you do for people in showing generosity is giving an opportunity for them to grow in quality. It adds value to themselves. Let's look at it from a biblical standpoint in Matthew 10:42.

Biblical Generosity

[42] And whoever gives one of these little ones only a cup of cold water in the name of a disciple, assuredly, I say to you, he shall by no means lose his reward.

Generosity comes with reward. What we often misinterpret in this act, is who should we look to for the rewards. On this path of studying, don't look to people to reward you for doing what you're capable of. Showing willingness and generosity to a person won't become personal when you know that your reward is coming from the Father. Generosity is a quality and characteristic of God. He will reward you, if you are a child of God. That said, generosity must become a part of your personality. Genuineness in this equation is always great because this quality is a matter of the character of the heart.

Let's define genuineness:

> "Possessing the claimed or attributed character, quality, or origin; not counterfeit, authentic; real; genuine sympathy; a genuine antique."

For you to possess something there has to be a change in your identity. It has to become real to you in order for you to have quality in your character and genuineness. It means you have to experience it and have experience with it.

Acts 20:30 reads:

> [30] In all things I have shown you that by working hard in this way we must help the weak and remember the words of the lord Jesus, how he himself said, it is more blessed to give than to receive.

For you to be able to give more than you receive, you need to come to the point where giving is more important than receiving anything in return. This applies to your time, valuables, or gifts. You shouldn't expect anything in return.

Depend on the most valuable organ in your body...your heart, for you to have fullness in this practice.

2 Corinthians 9:7 says:

> *⁷ Every man according as he purposeth in his heart. So, let him give; not grudgingly, or of necessity: for God loveth a cheerful giver.*

I love to study the topics in the Bible that help me to get specific proof about my walk with God. It gives me a better outlook on how to spend my time and energy in rebuilding myself. Bible verses can help you to understand the true meaning of giving or receiving. This is a great topic for Bible study. Use this teaching to help you on that path to freedom.

There is nothing wrong with getting help. Know who you're asking, who offers, and knowing whether generosity and genuineness play a role. Be aware of whom you're dealing with on your path.

IDENTIFYING THE SHIFT

GENEROSITY AND BEING GENUINE

Generosity and Genuineness as Value

Two examples in my life that I can use for this word are my parents. Growing up, I couldn't understand why they were so gullible. My parents would give away their life and it wouldn't mean anything for them. For so long they would feed, pray, and help you see your way through God's Words; pure genuineness. It wasn't until I was about 30 years old when I understood what my parents were fighting for. Seeing them give so much almost made me bitter against them. The simple fact that they gave until they had nothing left. I thought it was a waste on people.

If I could ever identify real genuineness, I'd say it's within my own family. My own parents taught me this valuable lesson. Don't you know that all the prayers they sent up for others and their children came back around and bless me? It was especially helpful when I found myself in places of need.

My parent are chefs. They love to cook and take great pleasure in it. They seem to even do it well under pressure. If you didn't get my drift, this was a big tool and a gift in generosity. They're relentless in the things they do for God's kingdom. Their gift of genuineness even through sickness, was an amazing thing to have first class seats to. Their naivety to people taking advantage of their gift was ultimately a seed sowed into the lives of others. My parents showed compassion with everyone. There are many values in generosity and genuineness if used in the right context.

COMPLETION
SH/IFT THE SIXTH

MAKING THE LIST

Making a list and personalizing it is the next step. Your list should contain everything in the areas where you are expecting success. Listing out the things you need to do will make life easier, more manageable, and less suffocating. This is a list of your personal goals and accomplishments to complete going forward to your destiny.

This is a priority. Feeling complete is the goal and to have nothing pending on your personal list. Your next list would be for your business and family. You'll want to document your future and it will depend on you completing your personal list. A key to completing it is to maintain your focus. To reach your purpose and destiny, you must be willing to do the work. You'll have to clean any messes you created, especially financial setbacks. Eliminate anything that will overwhelm you in making your future decisions. Target each specific area. Give yourself deadlines to meet. Check it off your list when complete a goal. Add a date to give yourself a sense of accomplishment and gather up the strength to complete the rest.

The Bible records in Habakkuk 2:2:

> [2] Write the vision and make it plain upon tablets, that he may run that readeth it. 3 for the vision is yet for an appointed time, but in the end it shall speak, and not lie; though it may tarry, wait for it; because it will surely come, it will not tarry.

Write your vision and make it plain. Then you can see and understand where to go and how to accomplish it. This is what principles are all about; setting goals and working on it, so that when the opportunity arises you'll be in a great place. There won't be any delays. Accomplishing your personal goals will make your business and family list easier to manage. You'll also gain experience for dealing with your next tasks.

PUTTING YOUR PLAN IN PLACE

After you've paid off all or most of your past bills and increased your credit score, putting your business plan in place is the next step. The hardest thing to do in this phase is recognizing the time it will take for you to know completely what it is that you're targeting. You'll want to determine the who, why, what, and where. Most of the time you're your toughest critic. Don't beat yourself up, just apply the same method you used in completing your personal list. If you don't meet your deadline it's ok this can happen. Set a new one as soon as possible. Don't worry, the goal is to finish what you started. The result is you feeling a sense of victory.

What am I saying, is that after you have gone through all the pain, hurt, losing people in your life, crying, screaming, and learning all these lessons:

WHY NOT GO AHEAD AND WIN?

WHY NOT WORK ON YOU?

WHY NOT PREPARE YOURSELF FOR RESTORATION?

Let me let you in on a little secret. This experience put my plan into place and brought me to my knees when I understood what I was preparing for and the purpose behind it. Have you ever heard the saying, "What you learn is also for others?" I didn't get it at first. I didn't understand it. When I got to the point of acknowledging that this wasn't just about me, but also for the ministry in me that would ultimately teach others. I could find the true meaning of not only putting my plan in action, but also activating the power of prayer over the plans. Everything you do in preparation is tied to your ministry. Understand that there is more in you than you know. This is very important for those who have a relationship with God. Know how to present your plan in prayer to your Father and cover every area of your life and ministry. If you accept the fact that greater is He that is in you than is in the world, then you shouldn't have any problems. As my bishop would say, your future will be so bright, you'll need shades to see.

LEARNING HOW TO PRAY

Having a healthy prayer life is important for everyone wanting to connect to God. It's good for you talk to God and set the atmosphere around you. It allows you to identify any damage surrounding you. The most productive prayer that covers all areas of your life is the Lord's Prayer. It speaks directly to God in the place where He resides. This prayer became a cornerstone for me after I got the full understanding of what I was praying about and why it was important for me to know it by heart. I practiced saying it every day until it became a part of my daily routine in my daily life. Prayer is a significant part of your identity. It is a signature to your walk on this earth and a reality check that you're still on progress to greatness.

The Lord's Prayer Matthew 6:13

> *[9]...Our Father which art in heaven, Hallowed be thy name.[10] Thy kingdom come, Thy will be done in earth, as it is in heaven.[11] Give us this day our daily bread.[12] And forgive us our debts, as we forgive our debtors.[13] And lead us not into temptation, but deliver us from evil: For thine is the kingdom, and the power, and the glory, for ever. Amen.*

Let me break down what this prayer is.

OUR FATHER WHICH ART IN HEAVEN:
The Being of the prayer, acknowledging who you're praying to and putting Him in His rightful place where He resides; the heavenly place on his throne.

HALLOWED BE THY NAME:
Giving praise and glory to the most high God to His name. The Father of the universe in His respective place and rights.

THY KINGDOM COME THY WILL BE DONE IN EARTH, AS IT IN HEAVEN:
I am waiting to see You and the place You have created for me. I will do Your will on the earth as You show me Your heavenly ways. I'll follow as You guide me.

GIVE US THIS DAY OUR DAILY BREAD:
Guide and protect me daily and provide for me food and shelter.

AND FORGIVE US OUR DEBTS AS WE FORGIVE OUR DEBTORS:
Forgive me Lord of my sin and when I do wrong in moments of weakness. Help me Lord to do the same and forgive those that mistreat me.

AND LEAD US NOT INTO TEMPTATION, BUT DELIVER US FROM EVIL:
Help me with my walk. Keep me safe from injuries that were meant to harm me and my family. Construct me in the times when I am tempted.

FOR THINE IS THE KINGDOM, AND THE POWER, AND THE GLORY, FOREVER AMEN:
I await Your coming kingdom, in all its glory and power. I acknowledge You coming to a world with all Your power, thank you.

I want you to understand that when you finish putting your plan in place, you'll need to activate the power of prayer on your plan to destiny through prayer. The enemy will show up and try to pull you into a trap to make you return to the places you're coming out of. If you believe in prayer, then you know that prayer gives insight into what is happening around you. It will teach you how to target problems moving forward.

Now that you know the Lord's Prayer to cover all the spaces of your life, family, friends, and enemies, SURPRISE! Yes, you have enemies, some of the closest people to you can become your enemy. Friends and some family can be a real threat, so praying and keeping your eyes open is the best thing to do. There is another prayer that is effective when you're sure that the enemy is planning to attack you. The enemy is relentless in his ways. Learn how to pray and wait for answers as to how to deal with those enemies in the form of people.

The enemy's antics are fatal with every move being intentional. The Scriptures record that he comes to steal, kill, and destroy. Even though that is the aim on your life, with prayer and supplication it won't succeed. At some point, you have to understand that without prayer, your protective walls can be breached. The enemy can take flight and launch verbal attacks toward you. But if and when it happens you will be ready, guarded in prayer, releasing a verbal block in the atmosphere around yourself and family. The enemy's wall is never weakened by the good you do around them. His defense is never weak. He'll use everything to come at you in full force; nuclear words that will kill you or damage your season. Sometimes these are people you may take counsel from. Keep confident in prayer and protect your pearls with the power of prayer.

Psalm 27 is also prayer that will cover and maintain you.

PSALMS 27

¹ The Lord is my light and my salvation; whom shall I fear? The Lord is the strength of my life; of whom shall I be afraid?

² When the wicked, even mine enemies and my foes came upon me to eat of my flesh, they stumbled and fell.

³ Though a host should encamp against me, my heart shall not fear; though war should rise against me, in this will I be confident.

⁴ One thing have I desired of the Lord, that will I seek after; that I may dwell in the house of the Lord all the days of my life, to behold the beauty of the Lord, and to inquire   in his temple.

⁵ For in times of trouble He shall hide me in His pavilion; in the secret of His tabernacles shall He set me; upon a rock.

⁶ And now shall mine head be lifted up above mine enemies round about me; therefore, will I offer in His tabernacle sacrifices of joy; I will sing, yea, I will sing praises unto the Lord.

⁷ Hear, O Lord, when I cry with my voice; have mercy also upon me and answer me.

⁸ When thou saidst, seek ye My face; my heart said unto Thee, thy face Lord, will I seek.

9 Hide not Thy face from me; put not Thy servant away in anger; Thou hast been my help; leave me not, Neither forsake me, then the Lord will take me up.

10 When my father and my mother forsake me, then the Lord will take me up.

11 Teach me Thy way, O Lord and lead me in a plain path, because of mine enemies.

12 Deliver me not over unto the will of mine enemies; for false witnesses are risen up against me, and such as breathe out cruelty.

13 I had fainted unless I had believed to see the goodness of the Lord in the land of the living.

14 Wait on the Lord; be of good courage, and He shall strengthen thine heart; wait I say, on the Lord.

DIRECTION
SH/FT
THE SEVENTH

HEALTH
CORPORATION

After you've learn how to pray and execute your plans, getting direction is the next step in this shift. Finding direction is about finding yourself. Putting yourself in the perfect place to see the path before you, but first you'll have to determine what that direction is going to be for you. Getting to that place means being open-minded and listening. There may be extreme highs and extreme lows.

The extreme highs are places where you raise the bar. Your listening ability is improved. What reveals itself to you in your daily life, while you're taking a walk or driving to work etc.?

The extreme lows happen when you put all that you have observed into practice to direct yourself in your desired place. Extreme care of yourself is a necessity. Your purpose depends on this because of where you're going. If you don't take the opportunity to take overall care of yourself, the extreme lows will pull or set you back. These extreme lows are isolation or depression. It can be anything that hurts your chances to act on the spiritual direction given to you for you to bring it out into the natural.

I have the perfect example about finding direction in your daily life and how I used it to condition my mind to self-direction.

The first car I bought with my own money was 2000 Oldsmobile Intrigue. It was an old car but I felt great about it. It ran well, took me anywhere I wanted to go. There is no greater feeling than when you achieve something on your own. I knew that this was going to be my "point A to B" car, but not before I understood the value of the car. I had to figure out how and what I needed to upkeep the car. This wasn't my first time with a vehicle, but this part was new to me. I didn't have to do this before because I had others who would. After few months, my car started to show me signs and I had questions.

Now as a woman I had no idea what to do. I had no interest in fixing this vehicle. I felt all types of stress. This was going to cost me. I had just moved to a new state, new apartment, and was working on my finances. I didn't need any more trouble. The costs just kept going up, but little did I know that this was a teachable moment. I was about to understand and learn a new direction. The vehicle issues awakened a spiritual place in me and taught me how to take direction properly.

The first thing I noticed was that the service engine light come up, then the low oil. Shortly after, it was the anti-lock brakes and low washer fluid. Now to most people this is a breeze, but I am not most people and fear begin to call my name. I started to speak in Jamaican Creole to God, "A wa dis pon me now pupa Jesus." In English it would be, "What is happening to me now Jesus?"

Surely, I thought that the enemy was coming after me and messing with me again. Was there no one else in this world? Why am I a target? Have you ever felt like everything you did just created another outcome that you just don't need at the time? I started to complain to Jesus to have mercy. Around the same time, I was also trying to save up for my first vacation because I had never been on one.

This lesson taught me value, how to use the direction, and how to direct it in the places that needed. I had to fix the source that created the problem. There was a need for me to understand when something is wrong and before damages occurred, use the direction and signs that were clear. It came down to identifying how to take care of myself conditionally.

IDENTIFYING THE SHIFT

SERVICE
YOUR ENGINE

There was one night that I couldn't sleep. I had to be up early for work the next day. The last thing I wanted to deal with, was being tired on a twelve-hour shift where I have to constantly exercise patience, generosity, and genuineness. My body was not cooperating with any sleep position or pattern. Some days, my back was speaking in unknown tongues that I couldn't understand, but the true interpretation was about to reveal itself.

Finally, my back pain took a turn since I was ignoring the problem. It was a week that my children were out of school and I took a few days off work. It must have been God because I was about to learn a new lesson on servicing my body. My back took me through a hellish type of pain. I refused to spend more money, even though the doctor prescribed medication that would relax my muscles.

Then my back expressed to me, "You think mi done? I just a come." Translation: service your engine.

The pain was unnatural with no explanation. It was like a stabbing pain of hatred from my back. You know, it was the pain you feel when you find out that the person you love doesn't like or love you the same way. It would go and come back stronger than before. I prayed to God for mercy and peace. I needed grace concerning this ridiculous pain sent from hell.

I thought to myself, the devil is liar trying to kill me prematurely before I finish my destiny. I thought it was all because I didn't service my body. I didn't take the directions given to me and make the necessary changes.

After about a week, the children went back to school and my back started feeling better. I understood how to add health for myself in my budget and how much extra I'd need to pay for medication. Then it all made sense to service your engine. Your body is your temple. You must treat it well and listen to it when signs are showing you that there is a problem. Pour care into yourself. Use the necessary tools and supplies to keep your temple serviced. Think about that. See your doctor to help you take care of your temple (your engine).

Service it with oil, meaning pray and read the Word. Make sure your anti-lock brakes are working properly, so that you can see the signs. Fuel your tank. Be consistent. Exercise breathing in the atmosphere and exhale all impurities. When you learn how to service and upkeep your engine, then the outer maintenance will become much easier. It will continue to transition you into your intended life direction. The possibilities are endless. Through prayer and understanding spiritual movement in your life create self-direction. It will put you in combat mode. Put on the spiritual armor. You'll never lose a battle if you learn how to armor up. The Bible tells us to put on the whole armor of God so that you can stand against the wiles of the devil Ephesians 6:10-11. When you have spiritual direction it's less likely for anything to come against you. Why? Because you will have a clear view of your ministry and where you're going. Before your desires become public, direction is the key that unlocks any door.

BUDGETING YOURSELF

Budgeting is a huge responsibility. Putting your money to work is your next to step. Bringing your idea into existence will take real budgeting. Your home, education, food, and personal expenses are all part of your budget. We all go through financial shifts. To be successful at stabilizing it, you'll have to balance your budget. Decide which the parts of your desire you're willing to fund first.

First things first, practice. Make sure that you're saving. Clearly monitor the monies you spend. Practice writing every expense down so you can see any messes you need to clean up. After you finish, pray about putting a plan together for a budget for every season to come.

Money management is very important in your shift, so as soon as you can, get good advice to properly prepare you for dealing with your finances and investment. It will afford you the chance to create opportunities. Debt can be stressful. The more information you receive, the more you can practice money management. Good money management can relieve stress. It can also strengthen your relationships. When preparing yourself for something as big as your future, a calendar may be a good idea. It'll help you stay on target.

Don't be afraid to challenge yourself in this shift. Your success depends on the obstacles that you overcome. Divide and conquer moving forward. This is a great time to start. The best thing about budgeting that I found is the opportunity to give back later. Every seed planted in money, friendship, or time are eligible for the laws of sowing and reaping.

Luke 14:28

> *28 For which of you, intending to build a tower, sitteth not down first, and counteth the cost, whether he have enough to finish it?*

Giving is never too hard for you to do when God is in it. You will find the that you have sufficient to give when your budget has a purpose.

I wanted to give back to the place that helped me grow into a better person in tithes and offering. I suddenly understood why budgeting was so important for future giving plans. My contribution is part of my covenant. It's a priority in my budget, an investment to bless, and to become a blessing.

FORWARD

SH⁄FT THE EIGHTH

OVERCOMING FEAR

Moving forward can sometimes bring about fear. There are different types of feelings that come with fear, anger, frustration, or frequent pain are some of the most common feelings. When you're experiencing a difficult time, it can illuminate everything; even your actions.

Fear doesn't always make sense. It's an unknown fear. This distraction will become real if you allow it. The only thing that can stop you from accomplishing your purpose and destiny is fear. It'll show up just in time when your life is about to change and distorts your view of where you are and how to get where you're going.

Fear is like a Silverback Gorilla takes you for a ride in the jungle full of defeat, dragging you around snake infested thoughts, and endangering your destiny. You gradually lose opportunities to elevate to excellence. Fear builds false reactions in you and will attack the very things sent to make you greater. It brings an illusion of what may seem or sound real. It can like a storm interrupting your life and creating a tsunami of feelings covering your view. Your thoughts can seem foggy and everything feels out of place.

The problem that we have is that we're always trying to remove fear instead of moving forward in despite fear. If we understand how to use fear to stretch us to our fullest potential, then the fear will inadvertently create wisdom for you to be better each time.

Can you imagine yourself riding on the back of a fearful beast? Sure, you can! Doing it would also bring some fears wouldn't you say? Just keep practicing. The fears of not accomplishing the challenges set before you'll make you even more fearful. Don't be afraid to ask for help. Work on things in the face of fear. Don't let fear bully you with lies. Put under your feet the annoying words that harbor in your mind. Use it to help you get better, and the things that make you upset. Fight for yourself and make your request known to God. Push past the defective words. They have no power to control the God in you. The Bible says that, "I am fearfully and wonderfully made by God."

The scripture tells us that fear shouldn't be an area of total focus. It's invalid and isn't an image that should be a part of us.

2 Timothy 1:7

> [7] *For God hath not given us the spirit of fear; but of power, and love, and a sound mind.*

The scripture exposes fear as not part of what was originally given to us. Some of our fears in life aren't personal, but intentional. The force behind it is to injure any progress you make in life. When fear shifts the rhythm of your heart, it can lead you into depression. This is where you need to get yourself ready to take flight. Elevate in prayer, change the atmosphere surrounding you. Fear is like acid; a contagious liquid that will spread and cause more damage, especially when others depends on you.

Fear can make your season the loneliest of your life or the best. If you can control how your day is going to turn out then fear has no problem with you. It's about control. If you are fearful but can resist the feelings, you'll learn a new way of dealing with fear as you encounter it. Take control of how it makes you operate.

Again, you can have success in this if you deal with the source. Where did this specific issue come from? How did it move from one person, place, or thing? What was the last outcome of your last dealing with fear? Find the source and you will see the outcome and the reason behind it. Remember, the only reason fear arises is to do damages. It has the same intention each time, no matter the situation. You can pinpoint every fearful action and make it a success.

Exposing fear is another method of dealing with it. Know what it is and how it affects you and others surrounding you. Fear is a spirit that cannot be seen. It can however, be identified in actions. Every fearful action brings an equally fearful reaction. Your thoughts that can magnify or minimize issues. It is your words that affect the thoughts. Your thoughts put fear in action. Be careful with your thoughts and words.

IDENTIFYING THE SHIFT

RELENTLESS FAITH

When dealing with fear, you'll need to have relentless faith. Fear comes to create harm, while faith comes with intent to build. Faith is especially necessary when you're going through a season where you're relying on strength. Having relentless faith is a personal choice. Although you can't see it, just like fear it can be displayed. The Bible speaks on faith as a substance; something of great importance and value of what you are believing for yourself or others.

Hebrews 11:1

> [1] Now faith is the substance of thing hope for and the evident not seen.

When going through fear, faith should be present. The substance that's needed is faith that you're hoping to be moved by faith evidence without seeing faith physically. Faith becomes a part of your identity. Anything that becomes a part of your identity takes practice. Practice staying focused on the things that will to take you through by faith. Communicate and elevate your expectations. The evidence is present in that action. It will work in any shift of faith present; whether in gain or loss.

Philemon 1:6

> [6] That the communication of thy faith may become effectual by the acknowledging of every good thing which is in you in Christ Jesus.

Having relentless faith in the middle of losses can be hard, but at this point you can't stop moving. It would be crazy for you to give up anything without the fight of faith. It's the best fight you will ever have to master, it speaks and professes good. It's a lifelong journey that will be display and minister to others.

1 Timothy 6:12

> ¹² *Fight the good fight of faith, lay hold on eternal life. Whereunto thou art also called and hast professed a good profession before many witnesses.*

When your faith becomes a witness, you'll fly past anything that could cause you to fall. Your faith can now become a hiding place in all area of your life.

Faith reminds me of another animal, the Eagle. The Eagle is a fearless animal. It soars through the air, targeting its prey using its extraordinary eyesight to zoom in and attack. Their eyes are among the strongest in the animal kingdom. Their eyesight is estimated to be four to eight times stronger than that the average human. The Eagle's eye can spot its prey around two miles and kilometer away. Considering that the Eagle can weigh ten pounds at a lightweight, their eye is said to be the same size of a human's eye.

This animal is by far the most interesting animal of all. It is the perfect example of when focus becomes a necessity and following through is crucial to success. This is how you should be in your faith. Attack every problem by maintaining your focus on the object. Have relentless faith.

People are often referred to as an eagle or use an eagle to represent their faith. Moving forward with clarity is a fundamental means of sharpening us to see anything in it's true color. To see an object for what it is; expected or not.

Praise is another form of displaying faith. Have you ever heard the phrase, "Praise your way through?"

Learning how to praise is the one thing we could be lacking in our walk with God. It's one of the most effective ways of professing faith. Praise and worship has its own identity. Set the atmosphere using praise and worship to God. You may speak in unknown tongues to invite the presence of God. Profess your faith to the Father. Reaching out to Him in that moment. When praise becomes worship, it's like the pureness of spirit meeting Heaven. This intimate time with God takes a little time. You can't make it a performance. It will cost you something. It will call for you to get up little bit earlier. Give yourself time to meet with God and turn your praise into worship.

WHAT IS PRAISE AND WORSHIP IN IT'S SIMPLICITY?

Praise gets you to access. Verbally expressing gratitude in the air. It makes a clear passageway for an incoming connection into the glory of God. Making a way for worship.

When worship happens, praise is an effective combination of known and unknown worlds collide. It shifts the atmosphere and anything that stands up against it. Praise is the rocket launcher that lifts, while worship takes you to the destination. They are two different words doing two different things, but work together to bring incredible results.

Having your own praise and worship is important for times when you're under attack. Using praise and worship as a defense mechanism, alongside scripture helps us to win attacks. Some of the same scriptures you may have heard as a child are the most powerful words to pray out loud in the atmosphere. It taught me how to step forward with praise into worship using God's Words and my faith.

Psalms 91:1-2

> *2 He that dwelleth in the secret place of the Most High God, shall abide under the shadow of the Almighty. 2 I will say of the Lord, He is my refuge and my fortress: my God; in Him will I trust.*

Learning how to trust in God's words will transform your faith. Your praise will transform into a real worship experience giving you peace in the middle of any circumstance. The Word will give you understanding and knowledge on how to thoroughly speak and create opportunities for God to shift in your life. Any unwanted movement toward you and your family will move according to your faith with praise and worship.

Psalms 91:5

> *5 Thou shall not be afraid for the terror by night; nor for the arrow that flieth by day. 6 nor for the pestilence that walketh in darkness; nor for the destruction that wasteth at noonday.*

It doesn't matter if it's day or night, praise and worship works everywhere and anytime through faith.

Psalms 150:1

> *1 Praise ye the Lord. Praise God in His sanctuary; praise Him in the firmament of His power.*

You can make any place a sanctuary. The moment you give God praise and glory in His name and His power, when you're using your faith.

Psalms 144:1

> *¹ Blessed be the Lord my strength which teacheth my hand to war, and my finger to fight.*

This tells me that my hands lifted in total surrender to my Father moves any situation. Understand that relentless faith is the only way to combat all your fears. Faith teaches us how to run with the wolves while maintaining your eagle status. If you keep in the air with praise and worship, you'll fly above the pack. Always keep prayer in the front. Watch closely to see the results of your prayer through faith.

Never underestimate what faith can do when you believe. Faith has a distinct sound that cannot be hidden behind voices. God will showcase your talents and gifts through your faith and restore you because of your faithfulness.

IDENTIFYING THE SHIFT

RESTORATION

I don't know about you, but I want to be fully restored. Restoration is a shift that paving the way to success. It can be like a new life or path to an open door. It's all a part of restoration, but it won't matter until you understand that restoration is really about your mind, body and soul. If there are parts of your life not functioning properly, you'll never experience true restoration.

To be fully restored takes true commitment to ourselves. Restoration is not only about our pocket prospering while other areas of your life suffer the damages from your newfound riches. Going after every penny is not restoration, especially if you're not disciplined.

Your mind is like your vehicle. It takes you everywhere and can travel distance without you being there physically. For example, you can be at work and your mind is all the way on another island. It can take you to places in your past and cause major build up. Your mind has the capabilities to download and reject information. You may often ask yourself what you were thinking. Questioning yourself using your mind to comprehend what took place You use the space in your mind that houses your memories to replay scenarios. I don't know how you would feel about this statement, but your mind is the most valuable tool you own. Why is it that you don't the take time out the clear your own mind?

Why is this tool box so heavy filled with tools that you're not using? When you get to this point, you've become mental hoarder. What is hoarder you ask? I am most happy to explain.

A hoarder is someone that never gives things up no matter how long they've had it. In this case a mental hoarder holds on to harmful information that can eventually decrease the health of your mental state. Holding on to destructive thoughts can cause you mental and physical problems. It funnels information through your body and your body responds like a car crash causing multiple issues. Your mind controls your body; your body houses your soul. Whatever you detect, you'll feel it in both your body and soul. Take care of your mind.

Romans 12:2

> *2 And be not conformed to this world: but be ye transformed by the renewing of your mind, that ye may prove what is that good, and acceptable, and perfect will of God.*

If you learn how to take care of your mind, then the body will show proof. Your thought process will change the way you process situations and transform. For this to happen, you must learn the art of communication and listening. Listen to the complaints of your body transmitted to your mind and soul. Accept the information given to become more proficient in your mind, body, and soul. Becoming skillful in your mind can help prevent harmful information from destroying your body and soul.

Corinthians 10:4

> *4 For the weapons of our warfare are not carnal, but mighty in God for the pulling down of strongholds.*

The strongholds created by your thought patterns will pull you into damaging attacks on your mind, body, and soul. Sharpen your skill in reading or researching an area of interest to challenge your mind daily.

In the previous chapter I talked about elevating in different areas toward personal growth. In this chapter, I'll share more on disciplining yourself in communicating and listening. I'll challenge you to discover things that set you back from walking into full restoration. Are you held back by your fear of the past or present? How do you deal with these things in your daily life?

One way is to control your emotions around others. Be fully in tune with your mind, body, and soul to understand clearly what's next. The only thing that can defeat you in these areas of life is yourself. Communicating and listening gets you more than halfway toward meeting your goals of restoration.

One of the ways you can tell that you're growing in this area is your emotional response to people's negativity as well as how you process it. Every day you can release your mind and relieve your body to connect with your inner man, breath in deep and let go of all that affected you throughout your day. Take time to unwind and spend time focusing on your purpose. You'll notice the difference in your daily actions. Some will be small, others great. You'll also start to be more aware of how you respond to your family, friends, and even adversaries.

One of the greatest keys that I found to restoration is listening before you speak. Let me share an experience I had with you.

I came across a magazine that caught my attention with a photograph of the Great Grey Owl, I didn't think anything of it until about two days later.

I went shopping in a department store to pick some supplies for my apartment, and there it was again. There were images of the owls everywhere; on towels, curtains, everything. I figured it was time for me to research this animal because there must be a reason I'm seeing this animal everywhere. Finally, after reading that initial magazine and doing other research, I found out that this species is a great gift.

The Great Grey Owl is said to be one of the world's largest owls. This special bird has spectacular listening abilities. Their hearing is so acute, they can hear creatures traveling underground.

**HAVE YOU EVER WONDERED
HOW MUCH FURTHER YOU WOULD BE
IN YOUR LIFE IF YOU LISTENED MORE?**

**HOW MUCH MORE RESTORED
WOULD YOU FEEL IF
YOU LISTENED MORE OFTEN?**

**IF YOU LISTENED, YOU WOULDN'T
GET INTO WRONG RELATIONSHIPS.**

**WHERE WOULD YOUR MINISTRY BE
IF YOU HAD LISTENED?**

**MAYBE LISTENING ISN'T YOUR PROBLEM.
WHAT IS? WHAT'S KEEP YOU FROM
BEING FULLY RESTORED?**

**COULD IT BE SEXUAL HABITS?
ARE YOU TRYING TO
FIND LOVE EVERYWHERE?**

**COULD IT BE A DRUG HABIT OR
ADDICTION THAT HAS YOU TRAPPED?**

**COULD IT BE THAT YOU DON'T
SPEND ENOUGH TIME SEEKING GOD?**

**WHAT ABOUT UNFORGIVENESS?
COULD IT BE THAT? WHAT IS THE PROBLEM
YOU NEED TO CONFRONT?**

**WHAT HAPPENED THAT CAUSED YOU
TO NOT BE FULLY RESTORED?
WHAT ARE YOU MISSING?**

Matt 11:15

> [15] *He that hath ears to hear, let him hear.*

Hearing and listening are spelled differently, but both have similar meanings behind it. To hear requires an action as well as, listening both spiritually and naturally.

When we talk about the mind, body, and soul in restoration, how it begins that matters, and the outcome you're expecting. Coming back to your natural self. Who you were designed to be. What was the natural state of your mind for your dreams and aspiration. What devices will you use to commit to yourself in this area? How did you download information before there were digital apps?

How did you interact with people before your relationship your relationship with God? Do you know who God is? I am simply saying get back to who you are. Identify and remember whose you are. Don't lose yourself, restore yourself.

Restoration is not about competitiveness in trying to keep up with others. Would you lose everything just to fit in?

Matthew 7:26

> [26] And everyone that heareth these sayings of mine and doeth them not, shall be like unto a foolish man, which built his house upon the sand.

What this verse is saying, is don't build your brand on foolishness, sandy places where you will sink. Sand doesn't stay in one place. It moves around with no control or stability. Sand can easily change shapes to fit and into things or take on the shape of anything.

The point to this title of Restoration is for you see that there must be a personal and spiritual shift in your life. You have to recognize that there are deep issues that can hinder your growth and clog how it connects to your overall person. It can delay how God shows up as a great factor in fully restoring you.

Do not be ashamed of Me or to speak of me for I Am the right hand of My Father. There is power in My name, says the LORD to everyone that believes in Me. I died for you. I laid down My life for you too, yes you.

I will bring you full restoration saith the LORD.

DISCIPLINE

Let's define discipline. Discipline is the practice of training to obey rules or a code of behavior; punishments are often used to correct disobedience.

Discipline is a personal project to work on improving you. This takes both patience and practice. When going through discipline, it can feel like you're through punishment. It will change your patterns. You'll find yourself observing your behavior and conduct with people, how you respond, and how people respond to you.

Becoming disciplined is a wide-open field for learning and forming new behaviors to enhance who you are or who you want to become. It can feel like you're punishing yourself. It's important that you become disciplined. It's a big part in keeping yourself fully restored. This is especially true in your actions the way you act and sound.

Some things can be misunderstood, especially when communicating with people you don't know very well. It's another thing to practice. It isn't just about your behavior, it is an overall shift. An extremely personal and intimate decision to change your life. Let us define practice. The Oxford Dictionary defines practice as the actual application or use of an idea, belief, or method as opposed to theories about such application or use.

In other words, to practice something, apply yourself. After reading this definition the word "theories" jumps out at me. I had to look it up too.

THEORIES: A set of principles on which the practice of an activity is based.

Practice principles based on the activities that will bring results. The change you seek all comes back to discipline. It's never too late to learn to apply principles that enhance who you're becoming. Your life and lifestyle will change because of it. What are principles?

Principle: A fundamental truth or concept that serve as a foundation for a system of beliefs or behavior or for a chain of reasoning.

Set a foundation for what you're expecting. Establish a system of behaviors within reason, to bring divine connection on your life. Your desire to become disciplined is a call from your purpose to go higher change is needed. It doesn't matter how great or small the purpose may be. If it's pushing you to become more disciplined, there's a purpose.

The scripture reads that a man named Paul was called to the office of the apostle.

Roman 1:1

> *¹ Paul, a servant of Jesus Christ, called to be an apostle, separated unto the gospel of God.*

For a man to be called to the office of an apostle, there should be a certain application of practice and principles.

The apostolic anointing is a divine calling on someone's life who has also practiced becoming disciplined and honorable as a warrior in his beliefs. They're someone that understands the true concept of practicing to become remarkable in his behavior. God honors His Word and finds honor in that person.

It takes discipline for a person to be received to this level of office. Gifted individuals can break strongholds off your life. Total obedience and discipline will open supernatural gifts to establish you in the kingdom of God.

Romans 1:12-13

> [12] For I long to see you, that I may impart unto you some spiritual gifts to the end ye may be established. [13] That is, that I may be comforted together with you by the mutual faith both of you and me.

If you take the time to become disciplined and allow God to impart His gifts to you both naturally and spiritually than there is a reward in that. God wants to be a part of your life. He has gifts that were promised to you.

What if all it took was you walking in discipline? Truth be told, we're better at trying to help someone else become discipline than ourselves, but how is that possible if you never get to point where you understand what true discipline is for yourself you never really practice? Practicing discipline is not like learning how to cook. While it's a good characteristic to have, it's not the same. Discipline will help you decipher the truth. It's not like putting a bunch of ingredients together to create a dish, switching out one herb for another just to satisfy your taste. In other words, there are changes that will take place that will irritate you and there won't be satisfaction until the ingredient is just right.

Dealing with issues you face, overcoming obstacles, and standing strong while building discipline will help you conquer some fears. When purpose and discipline become one, then there is calling. Make the effort to practice and place principle with discipline.

Have you ever felt like you were being punished for no reason? You were doing all you could, but it seemed like you weren't getting anywhere?

There is a reason for that. Start by finding out what it is that throwing you off track. Why aren't you feeling accomplished? It could it be that you're walking in disobedience. For example, for us whom are Christian with foundation based in a ministry, tithing is one of most common forms of disobedience. Some know how to, but don't. Some just refuse to, and most don't believe enough to. These examples can all be displays of a lack in discipline.

Proverbs 3:9

> *9 Honor the Lord with thy substance, and with the first fruit of all thine increase.*

We are lacking wisdom, knowledge, and understanding when we are always finding ourselves in disobedience. Discipline will never find us if there is no purpose to your change. Not having knowledge, understanding, and wisdom can bring serious consequences in every aspect of your life.

Proverbs 3:13-18

> *13 Happy is the man that findeth wisdom, and the man that getteth understanding.*

> [14] *For the merchandise of it is better than the merchandise of silver, and the gain therefore than fine gold.* [15] *she is more precious than rubies: and all the things thou canst desire are not to be compared unto her,* [16] *Length of days is in her right hand; and in her left-hand riches and honor* [17] *Her ways are of pleasantness, and all her paths are peace.* [18] *she is a tree of life to them that lay hold upon her; happy is everyone that retaineth her.*

Here's how I became disciplined.

I'll never forget the day I was being spoken to about how discipline will lead me to the right place. I got to work early that morning, and my client (and friend) decided it is not going to be a normal day. He was going to do what he wanted to do and no one was going to stop him. He was in control.

After about three hours I realized this was about to be another lesson for me to learn. He began to speak, "Dahlia here you go," he said. "Take this calendar." I took it and thanked him. Within the next hour he started to clean out a small cabinet full of calendars and postcards. I looked over the calendar he handed me. It had a road on the cover on one side and the road was covered with words. They were words of direction.

I interpreted it as God was giving instructions while on the road, but this was only practice. God is calling us to discipline when it is a major challenge. This challenge gave me the tools I needed for the spiritual journey to organize my life. I just had to see and keep God in it. I called it my calendar challenge.

My calendar challenge woke me up spiritually. It costs me about two hours of sleep, waking up every day around 5 a.m. to pray and have devotion before heading to work. That was my daily challenge and the most important of the five challenges on my list.

Are you ready to take the challenge? It's not a competition, but an opportunity to open the supernatural gifts of God for your life. Healing the sick, praying in tongues and interpreting, teaching the truth of God by speaking in the prophetic, seeing the miracles signs and wonders.

Hebrews 11:6 but without faith it is impossible to please Him, for he who comes to God must believe that He is, and a rewarder of those who diligently seek Him.

Diligence is discipline. When you get to a place where you're walking in diligence, you've aligned yourself in discipline. Diligence is having or showing care and conscientiousness in works and life. It's a constant effort to accomplish something; attentive and being persistent in doing it. Become a diligent student in discipline.

ORGANIZATION

Organization is part of the prophetic shift. This is a huge calling on your life. Organizing helps you to see your way on the track toward finishing goals and helps you to finish strong. There can be a lot of distractions keeping you from your destiny. Some of the major distractions will from people close to you, or from needs and wants. The important part to remember is that you need to stay organized to stay on your goals. Organize your true wants and needs.

Everywhere you look, there's a need or want. The children need your attention, the car needs maintenance, there's people you need to let go, gossipers, a heavy workload needs prioritization, you want a new pair of jeans, eating out, buying unnecessary stuff, this list could go on. It goes for the spiritual side as well. These distractions will derail you. You must organize. The true reality of the prophetic shift in organization is to stay on the trail so God can move. Stay focused on what God is doing in your life. Know that you may have to impart into others later.

Why is this a prophetic shift? It simplifies parts of your life and gives clear and spiritual instruction on what needs to be done. The prophetic shift calls for extreme changes in your organization. You'll have to break old habits and form new ones.

Mark 1:1-2

> *¹ The beginning of the gospel of Jesus Christ, the son of God, ² As it is written in the Prophets, "Behold I send My messenger before Your face, who will prepare Your way before You."*

Organization is necessary in this shift because the preparation is for the individual to master their way, and make a path for others to follow. As you're making your plans, know that God has instructed you as the messenger. You must be able to take instruction, experience it, organize it, and present it, before others can follow you.

Jesus organized a group of people and taught them. They followed Him and continued to learn from His teachings before they went public in their ministry. They gained experience as they followed him, put organization and instruction together, and worked to bring forth the church. Learn how to add and divide your time while dealing with distraction. Put into place dates and time to handle everything on your calendar without overloading yourself. Choosing to ignore this area organization will cause delays, and with delays, come more issues for you to work through.

WHAT'S THE PURPOSE OF ORGANIZATION?

Organization prepares you for harvest. It positions you to receive. It's important to know what and where you're going to invest as you continue in ministry or personal goals. Give yourself structure to finish the work you started. It gets easier to complete your goals when organization is the backbone of the plans on your heart. Get a full and clear understanding as to what and where to put your blessing.

This is a battle. It's critical that you teach others what you know. Get there first, by disciplining yourself enough to get it done. Overtake the area of your calling and effectively release it into others through thorough preparation.

The Bible spoke of Joshua, a servant of God displaying how to take instruction, organize, and apply. This strategy brings great results and victory for others that follow you.

You'll encounter people with cruel and devilish behavior that come off more resourceful than you. Stay one step ahead, be organized, be ready. We'll never see the full and unlimited resources of God until we attempt the impossible. We have to go for the difficult, hard, complicated things, that we can't solve without God's input.

For some people, organization is a gift, while for others it's a chore. The thing is, all your life you have been learning organization, but maybe this wasn't a priority because you didn't think you would really need it. You still have some knowledge of it even if you don't use it all the time. What if you applied some real practice into the principles you already have? How can you turn your failures into something useful? Never throw away your experiences.

ORGANIZE YOUR FAMILY LIFE

Family comes first. This is your first ministry. You'll never truly care for others until you understand how to care for your own. Communicate with them. Find out their needs and wants. It's not just about your vision; it's a family vision. Work with the kids on their future. Give them a vision and direction. Provide guidance and suggestions early. Teach them to organize and when to use their voice. In marriage, teach each other how to work on goals individually and collectively. Periodically check on the kid's goals as they'll need your help with follow-through. Make time for this. Carefully watch their grades and talk with them if there is anything that seems off. There may or may not be a problem.

Understand that children also get stressed and feel pressure at times. Be mindful of the way you speak to them, just because you're the adult doesn't mean they understand your feelings toward them.

Be compassionate to your family. Raising your voice doesn't always help. Find out the true story before you make judgement. Speak with them and address them by name. When children feel hurt severely, listen when they speak about any conflicts. True love begins at home; home is where your heart should be first.

Teach your children how to pray, especially in times when it seems like all their organization and plans make no sense. Encourage them to redirect and try again. Don't assume that because your child is silent things are ok. Things are always happening in their life and through their minds. It's better for you to know and address it with compassion.

ORGANIZE YOUR PERSONAL LIFE

Your personal life has everything to do with you. and how you treat yourself. Be mindful of who you let in your personal space.

Take care of your personal hygiene. It's not always a gift when someone offers you a mint. They may be trying to tell you something. Make your personal life your personal business to care for.

Change your perfume and deodorant from time to time. Being delicate in this area is a good thing. Go through your personal items and change something.

Purchase new undergarments to replace ripped ones. I know it might be your favorite. Married or single, treat yourself how you want others to treat you. Don't be afraid to spend a little out of your budgeting to enhance yourself. Change up your style every now and then. I'm not talking about the dollar t-shirt you like to wear to work. Wear something nice. You never know when the promotion is coming. The way you carry yourself may disqualify you. Change your attitude, smile, practice in the mirror if needed. Exemplify excellence. By now you should understand all of what you learn or fail at is a big part of your ministry.

ORGANIZE YOUR MINISTRY LIFE

Ministry is in everything you do in your life; the way you live, speak, and what you practice. Your personal ministry is your relationship with God and how he communicates with you. Spend time finding out what God has on His heart for you. That is personal between you and Him.

Romans 1:11

> *[11] For I long to see you, that I may impart unto you some spiritual gifts to the end ye may be established.*

Establish your relationship with the Father in all area of your life. Many times we desire to be in this area without knowing what it takes for us to have it. You must be patient for God to impart, teach, build, and establish you.

Ministry isn't like someone who doesn't know how to pronounce your name. It isn't about the small mistake you made when learning how to manage and obtain things imparted by God. It's so much more than that. People are relying on you to teach them how you made it. They want to be part of something great. Moving alongside someone they can identify with. Take your time with this. The Bible says that your gift will make room for you. When the time is right you will see how you should go minister. You want to have a mutual understanding about where you're taking His people.

Roman 1:12

> *12 That is, that I may be comforted together with you by mutual faith, both of you and me.*

The way you organize is dependent on what ministry you have. You'll need time and experience to put it all together. Every experience you have with God goes into your ministry; even your dreams and visions. The reason you're compelled to get your house in order is the call for true holiness. Holiness is total devotion to God! Turn everything over to God totally. His way may not be your way and total leadership may not be in your hands, but to follow Christ is to follow His leading.

There's always a person that can witness that God did it, but not before He confirms with you that He's doing this work. Ministry requires the supernatural intervention. If you follow God's protocol, you'll receive specific guidance that's in agreement with God's Word about how to reach His people.

THE TURNS

The turns that you make in your life will never become complicated if you understand that there's a purpose for everything. The turns most likely mean something for you.

My experience with going through turns opened my discernment with people and places. I discovered a deeper level of listening that seemed to never be wrong, but with that experience, an emotion feeling was attached. It was an ache that alerted me to be careful in some situations.

The turns you make in your life are going to be just a turning point. We're all so very different and learn differently. These differences will make it easier or more difficult because we comprehend things and download information.

What I learned about discernment is that it makes my turns a lot easier and helps me get out of difficult situations.

First, I want you to understand that I've been experiencing this for a couple of years. I just didn't know what it was, or how to use it. I started to notice that it would stop me from moving or speaking and teach me to listen more carefully to sounds and words. It allows me to listen and understand what is happening before and after a person speaks. I'm more aware of my surroundings and can identify who I am dealing with. It's important to learn your turns. Discernment has helped me many times and even saved my life. It's shown how much grace and faith work together.

Ephesian 2:8

> *8 For by grace you have been saved through faith and not of yourself it is a gift of God.*

The turns you make are important to your growth. It could be as simple as a body movement that ties into something that can change your mind or a small thought that keeps popping up frequently. There is something that speaks to you in a way that no one understands. That's what you should use to help create turns. Shift your life into something positive. It is your gift, use it.

Your turns can be a daily routine that evolves with force and time. You have to discern when it's happening. The activation of your discernment will cause you to move by of faith, vision, a dream etc. I want to share a dream that opened a turning point in my life me sensitive about things and how I discern when something is happening.

I had a dream about the five years ago that took me to a place with long halls. It was dark. I couldn't see or hear anything, but I could speak. What was the point of being able to speak if I was deaf and blind in the dream? I started to walk around silently. The walls felt rough and hard, like cement. While trying to find a way out of that place, I realized that I could smell that something odd. I move into the hallway, and turn into what seemed like an open area at the end of the hall.

I wasn't sure where the stench was coming from, but the more I walked the heavier the smell became. Immediately after making the second turn in the dream, I walked right into a skeleton dripping flesh. The smell knocked me out cold. I woke up out the dream and I was troubled. I couldn't understand why I wasn't able to use my sight or why was I deaf; especially since these were the most developed area of my walk with God. I was puzzled.

A few months later this dream opened in an area of my life that I never knew existed. It helped me to unlock my senses of touch and smell. Even though we smell and touch things every day, we are sometimes not sensitive to it. I realized that when I touch others I can feel or sense what going on depending on where I am spiritually. When I walk in any area, my sense of smell alarms me that there's a problem. It also shows me when the atmosphere changes and be on the lookout for trouble. As for me being blind and deaf in the dream it made me take caution in my life. Listening and watching became more noticeable in the way I viewed and took in my surroundings.

The point is that you never know what will make you turn or change or create motions of learning in your life that will help you and show a path that may be familiar. Soon as you take notice of it, your turns and choices will be different and changes will bring you. Understand these turns in your life and how important it is even when you're not taking notice of it.

TESTING
THE DESTINY
SHIFT

THE SWITCH

When you're about into walk destiny, you don't have the time to second-guess yourself. You have gone through training and now must rely on what you've learned. New people will take an interest in what you're doing and help to launch your ventures.

The true purpose of the new circle of people is to educate you and put your ideas to work. They'll help you see the ability of what you have been given by God in full effect. Most times, these people are already established in their careers and will understand the desires on your heart. Leverage them to pass down information that will bless you in this shift to prepare you for presentation.

This is where destiny meets reality and paints a picture for you. The Artist has perfected your craft and will set you on your way. The switch will go on and your light will shine bright.

I mentioned it earlier, but it bears repeating. My Pastor who is now an Apostle, said these words at church one day.

"Your future is so bright, you'll need shades to see."

The impact those words had on me were small at the time, but has since created movement on my heart.

When destiny creates movement, it can sometimes feel small and you forget about it. Years later it arises making it hard to recognize yourself. The changes will grow you into a different person. It will be noticeable. People will see the changes I and on you. Don't feel uncomfortable when you extend yourself. God will comfort you through it. Believe it or not, someone can speak destiny into your life and it can come alive if you're up to the challenge.

The Bible speaks of a young lady named Esther who was chosen for destiny. She was about to save lives and after numerous tests and purification, she became the wife of a king. In this switch, Esther met a young man that saw her truth and showed her favor to the king's heart. Of all the other ladies that were chosen for the opportunity, Esther was the one chosen by the king.

Esther 2:15-18

> [15] *"Now when the turn came for Esther, the daughter of a Abihail the uncle of Mordecai, who had taken her for his daughter, was come to go in unto the king, she REQUIRED nothing but what Hegai the king's chamberlain, the keeper of the woman, appointed. And Esther obtained favor in the sight all them that looked upon her.* [16] *so Esther was taken unto king Ahasuerus into his house royal in the tenth month, which is the month Tebeth, in the seventh year of his reign* [17] *"And the king loved Esther above all the woman, and obtained grace and favor in his sight more that all the virgins; so that he set the royal crown upon her head, and made her queen instead of Vashti.* [18] *"Then the king made a great feast unto all his princes and his servant, even Esther's Feast; and he made a release to the provinces, and gave gift, according to the state of the king.*

Understand what happened here. She was so favored that a feast was named after her. That blessed others as well.

Esther became the king's wife and the queen. She asked for nothing but the king's servant suggested and appointed a crown fitted on her head because of her humility. Esther was victorious, but with every victory and in any shift, there's always a price to pay.

To accomplish destiny the responsibility is great. When the crown is placed on your head, it's time to lead. Destiny brings a lot of things. Favors, comfort, or betrayal. Most of the time it's extreme. To complete it, you should be ready to shift when the time comes. The goal of destiny is victory.

The things that destiny brings are not going to be all in one area. You may experience it in the areas of your life that you want the most to work out. It will come from the most difficult and unpredictable areas of your life. You may have to confront the people that betray you with good character and communication to complete destiny.

Don't underestimate destiny. Yours could be tied to someone else's. You see it a lot in marriage, but it may be something completely different. It's yours to find that out and when you're in it, you'll discover the responsibilities that come along with it.

Luke 12:48

> [48] But he hath knew not, and did commit things worthy of stripes, shall be beaten with few stripes, for unto whomsoever much is given, of him much is required, and to whom men have committed much, of him they will ask the more.

If ever there was a person from a biblical standpoint that understood responsibility, I would say it was Queen

Esther. The Bible records that Esther received information concerning deception. There was a problem in the kingdom and God's people needed her help. She sent word to her uncle Mordecai for people to pray and fast with her for three days and nights. She sought God for favor and instruction concerning her immediate and extended family. It was her decision to appear before the king without being summoned. A very dangerous decision.

Esther took extra time preparing to present herself to the king, her husband. Requesting to speak with him put her at risk to be killed. Appearing before the king without receiving an authorized introduction in those days was trouble. Can you imagine how frightening this was for Queen Esther? Using wisdom, Esther decided the risk was worth the consequence for her people. As her husband shows her favor again, Esther shifted and asked her husband to attend a banquet that she would prepare.

Can you imagine the thoughts of the king, when his wife who knows the laws of the land, would enter his courts without being summoned? Esther wasn't the only one in the middle of destiny. The king was also about to shift after receiving information about the betrayal in his kingdom on his watch. It threatened to exterminate the bloodline of Esther, his wife and queen. The king gave Esther her request and saved God's people. He removed from his kingdom all the people that deceived him and switched up his leadership team. It saved his wife Esther and her extended family from extermination. Do see how destiny can collide with some else's. These two people, with two different backgrounds, individually and collectively, saved lives, their marriage and their kingdom.

Destiny can be as simple as a name that opens up something great in your life. The name Esther means star.

She shined brightly in her husband's eyes. Esther knew how to get to God's heart. This woman was a virtuous woman. She sought the true and living God and had continuous favor with her husband.

I have a perfect example how destiny collided with my life. I moved to Nebraska in 2015. It was an opportunity and opened a door. I took a leap of faith. I never saw it coming, but God was about to show up and show me the words the Apostle spoke in the atmosphere about my future being bright and needing shades.

These words were about to manifest in my life. Throughout this time, I had an encounter that led me to mean a young man named Arthur Lyles. He's a barber building his brand on principles he had learned. After about my third haircut at the barber shop, he scheduled me after his work hours were over. He was trying his best to fit in. He began to tell me about his journey and how God built him up.

Arthur may not know this, but he lit fire to words that the Apostle spoke into my heart that shifted me into a new drive finish this book. In addition, he passed on information as well as people who helped him launch the book. I read his book called The Cutting Edge and it has been lifechanging.

Destiny colliding with your faith and heart, light the way to other people's heart to invoke the things God places on your heart. I encountered a few people that taught me lessons that will continue to help me throughout this journey.

Destiny can be something as simple as a name, a quote, or some passage of information that will open something great in your life such as an idea, love, a small story or confirmation of a word.

The name Esther means star. A star is something that shines bright. It stands out and is noticeable. So is destiny if you recognize it.

I believe there is destiny in all of us. There's something good in all of us, but the choice to follow destiny runs deep. Find it and see it through.

THE ROUTINE BREAK

If I could convince you about anything, this topic would be it. Destiny will make you break routines physically and mentally. When health becomes an issue, physically doing what you're destined to do may be harder to accomplish. The last thing you need to be doing is fighting anything that has affected your destiny. Life is unpredictable, so taking care of yourself is a number one priority.

After doing some research on health issues, I found that this disease can keep you from completing what we desire to do. Cancer is one of leading cause of death in the world. It's slowly taking over multiple shades of people. Black, Caucasian, Chinese, Bi-racial this infection is no respecter of person.

It's of great important that you keep some routine in your life. You'll need it to fight and win some of the deadliest diseases out there that can be damaging to you both physically and mentally. They can put strains on your family, and prevent you from doing the things you're destined to do.

Besides cancer, there is an even more dangerous human immunodeficiency virus commonly known as (HIV). This disease has become too common. Having an honest, open conversation with your healthcare provider is the first step to a health routine. This discussion will give you a basic set of questions to ask.

You might not want to hear this, but you should be asking questions like how is this virus treated? How does one start treatment? What are some of the side effects? These questions and answers just may save your life and others.

Just like cancer, HIV is a killer of people's motivation, aspiration and dreams. There are people out there that are living with cancer and HIV, not because they didn't have a health routine, but because they may have missed the signs, there wasn't any proof that there was a problem, or nothing to identify any symptoms of something being wrong at that time. It's super important to know how and when your body is changing.

Diabetes and high blood pressure are another set of damaging problems; not to mention Hepatitis C. Follow up on your blood work with your doctor and ask about your blood type. Check on your heart, mammogram, obstetrics, gynecology and prostate are other necessary tests. Work with any specialists that your doctor may refer you to so that you have less to worry about.

Destiny has a routine as well. Make no mistake, your health is a major part of this. Having a healthy prayer life should be part of your health routine. Keep yourself, family and friendship covered. Learn how to pray and lean on God. I'm sure that after all the practice and lessons you've learned, you'll need direction and a clear mind for where God wants to take you. Understand the responsibility and requirement of prayer, as this is going to be a necessity. Like any other thing in your life that is dear to your heart, prayer should be a priority as well.

Prayer is a simple conversation with God. Becoming an intimate intertwining of the soul with Him, "beseeching the Lord." Prayer is that connection. It's a great place to receive answers to unanswered questions and keep contact with the Father. This is where you pour out your spirit. Have you ever pour out on God about a situation on your heart? Prayer is that quiet place where you can release. It's a remedy to a healthy life. Be prepared for the manifestation of your prayer in expected results, that will show up at the appropriate time. Having a healthy lifestyle will be a plus for long life and to complete what you're destined to do.

Destiny will have you breaking routines at any given time, but those breaks shouldn't come from trying to get to a healthy place. Your internal health is very in important through this process because we're human and we age every day. This objective of destiny will create movements taking you from place to place. Your body will be on that journey as well. Destiny changes everything and sometimes there are reasons why we are compelled to make those changes and adjust to what destiny is bringing.

Destiny also created relationship. The most important relationship is with yourself first. A real relationship with your health can have you feeling great about the addition relationships you entertain.

Breaking routines isn't just about how you take care of yourself. There can be other relationships, religious behaviors, habits and religion that you must break up with. Since destiny creates vision and partnerships, have a great attitude toward yourself. Others can shift you forward in your destiny and cause your routine to change. The multiple activities that can come from you walking into destiny can become overwhelming, but it's worth every moment; every unexpected moment. When you have stability in health, prayer, and your beliefs, when it's time to break patterns the effect will be mutual.

Breaking bad routines can launch you into destiny and a destination. Jesus had a destiny and a destination. He showed man what destiny and destination look like.

Fishermen become fishers of men breaking their routine to follow their destiny.

No matter how you see your life, destiny is on it. Prayer, health, beliefs, and religion is all but a small part of the bigger movement. What you have on your heart will grow you spiritually, unlock others with the same passion, and change the outlook on everyone's life. Destiny will cause a chain reaction breaking routines and fulfilling your life.

ADAPTATION

Adaptation is a form of redesign and reconstruction taking place to repair something. For example, repairing an area on a broken bridge. The broken area was the previous problem. Anything that is broken will need repairing wouldn't you agree?

So why is it that we fail to take the time to repair the broken areas? The breached areas are the sensitive places. They're the open wounds that are the damaged places in our life. Why is that these areas are not used to help you to reconstruct? Why is that we're defeated in these areas of our life.

It's important for us to have structure and to take the time to heal. Healing is a big part of our life and sometimes the process takes time. If you have to go through, when you take notice of the damages, it will be well worth the time and changes. When you have some time, it's important for you to accomplish something that you're destined to do. You can't go into it broken. You need to heal.

Repairing any type of damage requires some type planning. It's becoming our motto to say just give it time or time will tell. Ask yourself how much time do you need? When do you know it's time to move forward?

Following the desires of your heart and elevating to excellence will take you through reconstruction to be effective. Timing and healing is vital before setting out and giving your all.

Healing starts the repair and rebuilding of the foundation. For you to be able to move forward, you have to go back to the beginning where the damages occurred. Confronting those feelings will be your base. Accept what happened and move forward.

I can guarantee that majority of the time communicating and identifying the emotions, then connecting with it will help us to heal. The things we go through in our life help to shape our identity and how we identify with situations. It'll help us break down the cause and the effect it has on us. To get to the point of rebuilding healing is necessary. The broken places in your mistakes and troubles, requires healing.

True success is attached to healing, mentally, and physically. Internally, it changes your thoughts and relationships.

It restores, creates balance, it inspires, awakens, develops character, brings joy and fulfillment. There will be healing to the natural state of mind and your health. Reclaiming yourself and making you whole. This same healing is also spiritual. It's a movement of faith and your beliefs.

The Bible spoke of healing as the children's bread. When one woman activated her faith by asking God to heal her daughter that was vex with the devil. Her faith caused her daughter to be healed by the Healer Himself. A supernatural healing occurred b faith through grace.

Matthew 15:1-29 reads that it is by His stripes that we are healed. Christ was wounded for our healing. We are already healed.

Isaiah 53.5

> ⁵ *But He was wounded for our transgressions,*
> *he was bruised for our iniquities: the*
> *chastisement of our peace was upon him; and*
> *with his stripes we are healed.*

As believers, we know that Christ is a healer and by faith
we believe that we are already healed through grace.

Let healing illuminate, define, reconstruct, redesign, and
bring you to complete wholeness and truth. I believe that
everyone should experience healing. It is the path to
fullness and life. It's one of the substances that nurture and
help us move forward as well as rebuild.

IDENTIFYING THE SHIFT

DESTINATION

All of us have a destination, but I believe you have the power to control what the outcome is going to be. I don't know about you, but there comes a time when your main priority comes first and everything else will have to wait. The Bible says what would it profit a man to gain the whole world, but lose his soul. Your soul takes priority.

You're responsible for what's happening to your soul and how you respond to what its telling you. You can lose people but you can't afford to lose your soul. It's time to separate who you know from what you know, and what you believe. What you know may not be the truth and who you know may be the devil in disguise, but your soul should not be weighing in the balance. It's time to make a decision.

What you choose will have consequences. People are not your best option. The moment you choose to make a change, those same people will disown you. Your soul is dependent on you making the right decision. Your destination is final. The place God has called you to is also final. You only have so much time. It's imperative that you see your destination clearly in your life and where you're destined to win.

One of the things that forces me understand that destination is right in the middle of movement, is you may be in pain, anger or confusion. It will be that thing that enlightens you and awakens you to see the reality of your life. Why would I say that? Not everything you read is true. Everyone sees a different outcome of a statement and the truth, but your soul has only one outcome. What that outcome is, is totally up to you.

Habakkuk 2:1

> *¹ I will stand upon my watch, and set me upon
> the tower and will watch to see what he will
> say unto me, and what I shall answer when I
> am reproved.*

What will your decision be when you're rejected? What
would you do? How will your vision for your life change?
How will you set yourself apart and watch over your own
soul? What salvation will you choose? Who are you going
to turn to, now that people are no longer an option?

Jude 1:2-3

> *² Mercy unto you, and peace, and love, be
> multiplied. ³ Beloved, when I gave all diligence
> to write unto you of the common salvation,
> it was needful for me to write unto you, and
> exhort you that ye should earnestly contend
> for the faith which was once delivered unto
> the saints.*

Some things carry urgency and conviction for you make
the changes. For some of us, it's not the first time. It's
alarming us that the time is now. The shift is now. That
identity change is now. Being cultivated into God's image
is now. Walking in your purpose is now. While there are
many obstacles and private obligations for your life, the
time is now.

Jude 1:20 and 25

> *²⁰ But ye beloved, building up yourselves on
> your most holy faith, praying in the Holy Ghost.*

²⁵ To the only wise God our Savior, be glory and majesty, dominion and power, both now and forever.

Where is forever for you? You say you don't want to live forever, but what if forever is an option? Even if you don't know, is it as simple as when you die, it's over? Do you know for sure? I'm assuming your answer is yes. Tell me why we still dream? Seeing some of your dreams come to pass. Is it safe to pay attention to some of our dreams and leave the others? Or, could it be that there is a force behind it? The question is what's that force? What do you believe?

I completely understand how difficult it is to believe in anything without proof that it really exists. By nature, we are dreamers and visionaries. Our belief systems work best with our eyes. Your eyes are not the only thing that tells us that something exists without seeing it. For example, the wind. You can't see it, but you can feel it. You can feel the difference when it shifts into a different direction.

Maybe when particles of dirt or debris is added to it, you can see a form or shape. How about your sense of smell? Have you ever smelled something but you don't see anything to match it? You know what it is because it's not the first time you have encounter the smell. Isn't that proof enough that there is more to what we can see? What we know to be true is because of our experiences and knowledge.

Just because you haven't see heaven or hell doesn't mean that it doesn't exist. The more knowledge you gain in life opens your reasoning and quest for the truth. It is the truth that will give you peace and set you free.

Ecclesiastes 1:14 and 18

> *[14] And I gave my heart to seek and search out by wisdom concerning all things that are done under heaven: this sore travail hath God given to the son of man to be exercised therewith.*
>
> *[18] for in much wisdom is much grief: and he that increaseth knowledge increaseth sorrow.*

The more knowledge you gain, the more you understand. Do whatever you will with the knowledge you gain, but the choice remains for your soul and your destiny. Tell me how would you feel if you knew that the information you received was wrong and you're maybe lost. The outcome you receive may not be what you desire, and at this point it may be too late.

Revelation 2:7

> *[7] He that hath an ear, let him hear what the Spirit saith unto the churches, to him that overcometh will I give to eat of the tree of life, which is in the midst of the paradise of God.*

All of us have a "what if" motion. What if I had chosen to go right instead of left? What if I had listened? What if this motion is your last? To make preparation for your soul, what if this is the identifying moment to see God? The real force being the mystery of your life. What if this is the call to an identity change for your soul? What if this is your defining moment? What if? At some point, we will all experience death and your soul will have its own experience.

The Identifying Shift is an individual shift. It's all about your walk, your decisions and your accountability. It's of great importance to understand and study the path that you're on. The shift in our lives create moments of opportunity. Opportunities to simply awaken areas in our lives that we may not fully comprehend. The changes behind your identity, the force behind who we are and who we are called to be, the reasons and purpose for your existence and your experiences. It's all for you to figure out. The why's and how's are there for you to identify and use it.

YOUR DESTINY IS WAITING ON YOU TO SHIFT.

IDENTIFYING THE SHIFT

DAHLIA DOYLEY

Copyright © 2017 by Dahlia Doyley - All Rights Reserved.

www.ingramcontent.com/pod-product-compliance
Lightning Source LLC
Chambersburg PA
CBHW060800050426
42449CB00008B/1466